MICHAEL ROSE

VISITS

'Reality defies the wildest imagination'
-Lester Ross

FIRST VISIT

It was a grey afternoon, in a grey suburb of the big grey city.

The parking lot was almost full, and, besides, I wanted to park my inconspicuous car in a remote spot. I circled around till I finally found one. I parked with the back to the wall, the license plate not accessible to any viewer. I took my 'special effects' briefcase containing whatever needed to give authenticity to my image, opened the umbrella to protect my head from the light drizzle and started walking towards the building.

I entered the wide entrance of what used to be, in its glorious past, a grand mansion. Many nights it was the entrance to laughter and happiness, dancing balls and sumptuous suppers, in the romantic lights and shadows coming from the beautiful candelabras. Now, in the bright, but cold light emanating from dozens of fluorescent lights, the inside was crowded with an amazing combination of humanity's rejects.

I just stepped into the Memorial Municipal Hospital for Mental Disorders, known as West Side Loony House.

It was the start of my new assignment, an assignment in which I had a personal interest.

I had fought very hard to get it.

Ultimate top secret surrounded this assignment, as it had the potential to touch and shake the highest echelons of the Administration and the very foundations of the entire political system. Nobody was immune to this investigation, not even the President of The United States. It meant to get to the roots of every possible tree of knowledge, to get the true story of the tragic events which took place on September, 11, 2001.

One of the leads, a potential source of information, was my old buddy and soul mate, Lester Ross. This was the assignment for which I fought; to investigate him.

I truly believed to be the best person to do it, having known him for so long and having shared together so many experiences. They looked as adventures now, after so many years, but the element of personal danger was there, enough to bond us for the rest of our lives.

Evidently, he had some information about these events not known to anybody and he was not sharing it with the ones above him.

Moreover, he had disappeared from under the radar, after his wife called the Office to inform he is sick and would be absent for a while.

The very first few steps led me into a world completely different from what I have known so far. It was a world meant for the poor and destitute, as most public mental wards are everywhere. A policeman and few male attendants were trying to control raging, yelling, crying, and shouting, ragged people, who did all this in swirl of languages, some their own invention.

I made it to the main attendants' station, its green paint fading and peeling, with some broken benches full of waiting people. I went straight into a tiny office attended by a male nurse sitting behind a scratched old metal desk, his feet on its paper-loaded top. He was reading a newspaper.

I took off my overcoat. Underneath it was a white medical coat with my name, Dr. Robert Savoy, Mental Health Dept., embroidered on the upper left side. The attendant, his head buried in the sports section, was still ignoring my presence. I picked up a pile of folders, raised it with both hands, and banged them loudly on the metal desk, its vibrations jarring the male nurse to his feet.

"What the hell..." he started shouting, then stopped in the middle of what was supposed to be a following curse, after noticing my coat.

"Is this the way you are watching mental patients?" I started my attack.

No answer.

It was fine. I made my point of being the superior and catching a subaltern neglecting his duties, putting myself above and pushing him into a defensive situation.

I put my briefcase on the desk under his nose, opened it and started looking for a folder, giving the attendant the opportunity to satisfy his curiosity and glance inside. A stethoscope and a first aid kit with a big green cross on its top were visible. I pulled a folder and fished some documents out.

Presenting my credentials, as well as a letter of recommendation from the hospital's Director of Administrative Affairs, I made my request. In short sentences, I told the attendant I was there to see and evaluate, in complete privacy, a patient named Lester Ross. His family requested my recommendations in order to find a more adequate place for treatment.

Still embarrassed, the attendant did not waste any time trying to delve deeper into the purpose of my unscheduled visit. He buzzed for a junior attendant to escort me to my patient. While waiting, I snatched, unceremoniously, my documents from his hands and put them in my coat pocket.

I followed the junior attendant through the maize of corridors, temporary settings in what used to be the grand rooms of the mansion. Every few steps he turned his head back to see if I follow him, ready to intervene if any patient tried to harass. He had noticed the respect the main attendant showed me and tried to be as courteous as possible, assuming I must be a senior medic.

We passed through a large dayroom crowded with people pacing back and forth. Most of them were talking to themselves, a few smiling with an empty look, like staring at a friend hovering above, some gesticulating wildly with their arms thrown in the air, and others bending and picking up invisible trash from the floor, bringing it solemnly to the garbage bin affixed to the wall. A lot of imaginary fly catching. Disheveled hair, torn clothes, and drooling saliva created a nightmarish tapestry. I made my way through this collection of miserable people as fast as I could, trying not to touch or be touched and not to attract their attention.

While walking I was thinking about the hell I got myself in. Did Dante visit such a place before he wrote 'El Inferno' with his famous allegories about the purgatory?

These people were *crazy*.

We descended a flight of metal stairs into the basement, which was divided into more than a dozen small, completely secured rooms for the dangerous cases. We stopped in front of one of them. The attendant opened the door with the key fitting the lock from the outside only and pointing at a red panic button, told me to use it when I was done or if I needed any help.

Afterward, the door was locked behind me, and I thought I was left alone. Then, in front of my eyes was Lester.

He was stretched on his bed—a very strange bed that was even higher than the regular hospital beds, a bed to let you know that you

5

are in for a rough ride. It had leather straps on both sides, used to hold Lester tied to the bed in a position where he could move his head, but not his body.

I stood still, watching him. Same Les I remembered except the unshaven face and disheveled hair, giving him the appearance of personal neglect.

For a while nothing moved. Then his eyes started turning slowly sideways into my direction and, finally, locked on my face. A sudden light lit his eyes and the aimless wandering became a concentrated look of amazement.

"What the hell are you doing here? How did you find me? How are you doing? Am I dreaming?" The questions kept coming, his voice expressing surprise and happiness. It was, by far, the only sane voice I had heard since stepping onto the premises. Then, pausing in the barrage of the questions, he said; "Get me out of this contraption, please."

I undid all the ties and clasps and he slid with his feet down onto the floor. He stood up, looked at me, and with a sudden jump planted himself in front of me giving me a long strong bear hug.

"Robert, you don't have any idea how happy I am to see you. Wait a second. What do I see on your chest? Dr. Savoy? Wow, wow, wow. Since when have you become a doctor? What kind of doctor?"

"Same here," I said, my voice choking with emotions, real ones. "And to answer your other questions, yes I am a doctor, actually in clinical psychiatry. I had a middle age change of careers, but I'll tell you about it later. Now I am a resident in this establishment. Today, after coming back from my vacation, I found your name in the new in-patient list. It is useless to describe my surprise. You'll have to tell me what the hell is happening here, because if I know one sane person, it would be you. Nobody can convince me that you are mentally sick."

He looked at me and asked with a concerned voice; "Don't I look, act, or talk crazy?"

"Of course you don't. Not only that, but I'll get you out of here in no time," I said.

A look of horror replaced his joy and he said with anguish; "Robert this is the last thing I want you to do. Don't even dream about it. I need to be here. This is the only place that can give me temporary safe shelter till I find a better solution to my problem—a better place to hide."

He whispered the last words into my ear, his body bent toward me while his eyes made a slight movement upward, indicating that somebody was listening to our conversation. Anybody watching us, or even listening to the last dialogue, would have taken for granted this was a classical display of paranoia, schizophrenia and bi-polar behavior. But I knew he was completely sane, with good reason to behave this way.

The stingy, hidden motions with his palms indicated not to say anything somebody might hear and not to act in any way different than the way a therapist or an acquaintance might act, in case somebody was watching us. I had noticed the peephole before I entered his cell and I knew it was possible to be watched from outside.

I took the hints as they were meant.

We spent a few more minutes together, then, looking at my watch, I cut the visit short, saying; "Les, I'll have to leave you now to complete my rounds. But, I'll be back tomorrow, and if the weather is half decent, we'll take a walk outside in the garden. Let me strap you back in now."

I strapped him in with his full cooperation, and a minute after pressing the button, the door opened and I was out.

Stopping at the main attendants' station before leaving the building, I left instructions to remove him from any restraints, but keep him in isolation and under visual supervision till my return.

I just accomplished the first stage of my assignment—to create friendly contact and raise Les's expectations to meet again; he was a person in a menacing environment and I was the only friendly ally on enemy territory.

When I got to my car, I removed the white doctor attire, replaced it with a high clearance badge hanging around my neck, on top of my navy blue silk tie which matched my light blue shirt and dark navy suit. I took the forged letter from the hospital administration and folded it carefully, putting it in my jacket pocket to be shredded later in my documents shredder in the office.

Driving, I was overcome by vivid memories of my long friendship with Les—memories of distant times and distant places.

I parked the unmarked Government issue vehicle in my reserved spot and entered the large entrance of the building with its blazon in the middle of the floor, the eagle spreading its wings proudly under the name of the establishment. I scanned my security badge and then my fingerprints under the supervising eyes of the uniformed security personnel and entered the corridor leading to my office.

As I sat at my desk, my mind kept wandering into the past, bringing forth vivid memories—memories of Central America some thirty years ago…

I was a young executive then, barely out of school, recruited by a large European pharmaceutical company.

Why did they choose me?

It was a mystery for a long time and only a series of unfolding events later in life revealed the real, surprising answer. I had, indeed, some analytical skills, accompanied by schooling in the new and emerging discipline of Business Administration. I earned a degree from a good Graduate School, sponsored by what was considered state of the art in the field—Harvard Business School and Fontainebleau Economic Institute of Paris. The truth is, however, I was an average student. It was mainly because I had been steered into the business direction in spite of my lack of financial aspirations and accomplishments. Even a short academic career as an assistant professor in one of the disciplines taught at that Graduate School, although a successful one, did not add to my understanding of the real business world. Some entrepreneurial and business skills existed within me, but remained completely dormant and buried by my strong preference for social studies, mainly psychology and history. In addition, I was inexperienced, not exposed to the realities of life, my sheltered upbringing barring me from any life enriching lessons.

My superiors were patient and indulgent to my mistakes and lack of experience. The immediate supervisor, who had a powerful position in the corporation, gave me every chance possible and took me under his protective wing. His authority became mine, minus the official and burdening daily responsibilities which accompanied it and were carried by him. He became a mentor and source of inspiration, introducing me to the new world of hands-on management of a corporation.

After a very short stint at the company's headquarters, the gods smiled and a brush of real luck touched me.

That was the way I was thinking then.

Otherwise, how could I explain that a young, inexperienced, and special talent-lacking guy like me could be given such opportunities? Starting as a junior executive, I was pushed and shoved rapidly from one position to another, catapulting higher and higher in the corporate hierarchy. At the same time, the company itself was experiencing a rapid growth, fueled by its successful products, becoming a player in the international market.

I found out, much later in life, it was an inaccurate version of its special status and success and that its scope of activities expanded way beyond the known ones.

Before I knew it, I was given the position of Sales Manager and the assignment to develop the market for our products in a virgin territory for the company, Central America. When I called some of my friends to tell them the good news, I was surprised to realize that only few knew Central America is actually a distinct geographical region, a land bridge south of Mexico connecting North America and South America and encasing the Caribbean.

Six countries were included in my new frontier: Panama, Costa Rica, Nicaragua, El Salvador, Honduras, and Guatemala. Some of these countries were known as the birthplace of the notorious expression "Banana Republics," which defined their political systems—unstable, corrupted and influenced by foreign interests.

It was an uncharted assignment without any specific rules or targets. I was given an unlimited budget and business expenses allowance. My mission was to spend as much as I wanted traveling from one country to another within my territory, creating contacts by wining and dining prospective clients, suppliers, and potential local employees.

Periodically, I had to report to the top management, providing a progress report, profiles and personal data of some of these persons, based on a list supplied by headquarters. Some of them were not the kind expected to meet within a business frame of activity, but I was not in a position to be critical about the headquarters' choices.

Eventually, my trips started to bear fruits and I was told by my superior that a list of new clients for the company's products started to form. Suppliers of raw materials and services were recruited and a small nucleus of continuous activities was formed, bringing an aura of success to my efforts in the region.

Within less than a year my star was shining high in the company's constellation.

Occasionally I was even offered the privilege to use the company's business jet, whenever it was not engaged by the senior management in one of their mysterious and unaccounted trips, when very few knew where the bosses were. I could not understand how such a corporation could spend the enormous amounts of money needed to own and maintain a private jet, including two pilots on constant duty.

I found the surprising explanation years later, together with some other astonishing revelations, but who was I then to question the spending habits of my bosses? Besides, in spite of the unpleasant, claustrophobic feeling of flying at high speeds in the small cabin of a narrow airplane, my landings in the small airports of Central America, where each arrival and departure was noticed, gave me a lot of local clout. I was the high flying, young and successful businessman who arrived to spend lots of money.

Many times on my frequent visits to headquarters, when settling my travel expenses with the accounting department, the bean counters used to ask me, half jokingly, but completely envious; "Why don't you spend more? Are you on vacation?"

I had the feeling, in a way that my efforts were measured in direct proportion to the amounts I spent. I started telling my family that my hands-on management became cash-in hands management.

Later on in life, I understood the reason for this generosity and lack of monetary restraint.

I made quite good use of this blank check written to me. For the first time in my life I was exposed to wealth. Luxuries that a short time ago seemed far away and unattainable were offered to me on a golden tray with a silver spoon. I traveled almost every day to a different country within my territory meeting interesting people. Some were smart, some were funny, but each new encounter enriched my experience and added another shade to the tapestry of relationships I had created. I met entrepreneurs, dreamers, crooks, as well as bright and talented locals, eager to share with me their knowledge and skills.

Even after so many years, I remembered a real character that was a study in vanity and arrogance. He was, supposedly, a professional tennis player, although I never saw him in action. Tall, wiry and with muscular arms, he was, most of the times, dressed in white pants and a tennis top, sporting a racquet over his shoulder. When, one day, I asked for his address so I could send him a brochure, he answered with complete sincerity;

"The only thing you need to put on the envelope is my name, 'Orlando Antonetti, Central America,' and I'll get your letter; everybody knows me." I met him again few years later in the States, after he called my office asking to meet with me. By then he was a beaten man, his beautiful, voluptuous wife had left him for another woman, and he was unemployed and completely deflated from the airs he had assumed when I first met him.

Logistically, my center of operation was located in Managua, the capital of Nicaragua. The city is located in the middle of Central America, which gave me easy and fast access either south to Costa Rica and Panama or north to El Salvador, Honduras, and Guatemala.

Its airport, Las Mercedes International, consisted of one runway, used for both takeoffs and landings, and a very small building containing everything else: Customs, military border patrol, the only gate, used for arrivals and departures, the kiosk with souvenirs, snacks and drinks, the very few airline counters, and all other related services, extremely limited in their scope. Arriving airplanes taxied slowly, getting as close as possible to the building- where passengers descended down an ambulatory staircase and made their way to the gate, on foot, in scorching heat and blinding sunshine or tropical rain showers. Outside, a small line of dilapidated vehicles with cracked windshields, torn seats, dents, scratches, and stationary windows represented the only taxi fleet in the country.

A little shoe shine boy, not even a teenager, doubling as a gofer—a permanent figure in the terminal—became my main assistant in the building, forcing the luggage from my hands and taking me proudly from one counter to another when needed. I anticipated his smile when he spotted me, arriving or departing, while he anticipated my small contributions to his pocket. Knowing the cash tips went to support the family, I used to give him additional little personal presents, a trinket here, some candies and chocolate there, which brought him closer to his young age.

Nicaragua, conveniently located in the middle of Central America, has been a magnet for American intervention and influence for more than 150 years. It started with an American adventurer, Walker, who, together with a few hundred mercenaries mobilized from the human trash of California's gold rush, conquered the whole country and proclaimed himself its ruler. He became the President of the country for a short while but had to pay a high price for this honor, his head, which was taken away from him few years later when he was executed in neighboring Honduras.

There were plans to dig a canal through Nicaragua from the Caribbean to the Pacific coast going through Lake Nicaragua, which is right in the middle of the country. I was surprised to find out that this lake is the only body of sweet water in the world where sharks roam freely underneath the surface.

Panama was a better choice for this project and Nicaragua remained almost untouched for many years afterward, watching with envy at the prosperity the Canal brought to Panama.

The United States started to vest interest into the country by endorsing and supporting a hierarchy of dictators, after the American government got rid of Sandino, a Nicaraguan rebel who became its leader. He was not enamored with the Gringos, and these sentiments sealed his fate. Sandino succeeded in sending the Marines back home, but for only a short period; they came back and with a vengeance.

A new generation of tyrants replaced him, and this time the Americans were invited back with their interests fully protected. The father dictator and later the son, Anastazio Somoza known as "Tachito," became complete rulers of the country, in a fully traditional medieval, feudal way. A famous quote was attributed to President Roosevelt and later to President Truman about Somoza, the father, "He is a son of a bitch, but he is *our* son of a bitch."

After he died and found permanent rest in the family plot in Miami, Florida, rather than in his homeland, the keys to the Nicaraguan land and people were given to his first son, Louis. When he too joined his family mausoleum in Miami, the other son, Anastazio Somoza, was handed the dynasty's fortune. The younger Somoza was American grown and educated, a graduate of West Point, and he spoke English more often and better than Spanish. He was a pure capitalist whose purpose in life became to enrich himself, his family, and his associates at the expense of his own people.

Meanwhile, the fall of Cuba into the hands of Castro transformed Nicaragua into a battlefield of influence and international intrigues. A leftist underground, inspired and supported by Cuba, emerged and flourished. It was named, not surprising, the Sandinistas, after the only head of the nation who had objected the American dominance and control. Its mysterious leader, surrounded for security reasons by a heavy cloud of anonymity, inspired the younger generation. Comandante Zero, as he was known, became famous and adored by the masses, second in popularity only to Che Guevara.

When Somoza tightened the internal security, Comandante Zero fled to Costa Rica, but the movement continued to grow and tensions became palpable.

A major earthquake hit the country in 1972 obliterating Managua. When all following tremors ended, it seemed a powerful nuclear bomb exploded, reducing the city, especially its commercial and residential center, to an ocean of rubble, debris, and dust. It stayed like this for many years, as a major geological fault goes through it and the event could repeat itself. More than 10,000 people were officially declared dead, although the actual number of casualties was much higher.

Survivors fled the city, and it became a ghost town surrounded by collapsed buildings and mounds of debris, waste, and garbage. It was rumored most of the dead bodies were thrown into the neighboring lake, Lake Managua, which became muddy with all the debris and waste dumped into it, in addition to the regular toxins which found a permanent home in the lake.

I heard about this devastating quake even before I became employed by the pharmaceutical company or knew where the country was located, not ever dreaming that one day it would become my temporary home. For weeks, the newspapers described the rescue and then the search and recovery efforts, together with the misery and suffering of the population. Many nations sent first aid shipments of medications, food, and clothing, on top of large amounts of relief and reconstruction funds. They found a shorter way straight into the deep pockets of the rulers, Somoza being the main beneficiary. Only a small, insignificant part, far from making any impact, reached the people in need.

Later, when I started visiting Guatemala, I was overwhelmed by the contrast.

Guatemala City was hit by a major earthquake a few years later, which caused serious damage to the infrastructure and the buildings in the city. Yet, not too long afterward, it was hard to notice these damages. The rapid recovery, cleanup, and reconstruction were remarkable. People went back to their daily routines, life was going on as usual and only stories were left as a reminder of the event. This contrast helped me understand later, together with other factors, the undertow of dissatisfaction in Nicaragua and the slide towards a civil war.

Very few buildings escaped total destruction in Managua. One of them was a hotel, the Intercontinental Hotel of Managua.

It was built in the shape of a pyramid and its design saved it. Located at the top of a hill, it overlooked what used to be downtown, now an ocean of debris and ruins which ended with the view of the muddy lake.

It was said that Nicaragua does not have many roads, but all of them pass through the hotel's lobby. This hotel, the only one left in Nicaragua after the earthquake, became famous thanks to one of its occupants. It was the last residence of Howard Hughes, the first American billionaire and the weirdest of them all. He took over the whole upper floor of the hotel and barricaded himself, together with his Mormon caretakers, in complete isolation.

But besides Howard Hughes, the hotel was also known as the place where one could see mercenaries and arms suppliers conspire over lunch by the poolside, journalists trading rumors while getting drunk all day long, diplomats and government officials, Somoza included, gathering for receptions, adventurers plotting who-knows-what, and hunters preparing their killing gear, getting ready to hunt in the surrounding jungles. It was the only place in the country, except private affairs, where the local senioras and senioritas could display the latest fashion imported from Europe and the States, promenading in the lobby.

Outside the hotel, scores of small children, in dirty torn rags with their little hands outstretched, would accost any foreigner venturing out, begging for small change. They were persistent; the hotel guests were the only hope to fill their empty stomach. A few coins or one Cordoba soiled bill could bring lots of smiles and gratitude. Later on I made a habit of driving to the local McDonald's, where many children were hanging around, looking with envy at the privileged customers stepping inside. I would go in, order a dozen burgers and fries, and bring them out, placing the food into their grateful hands.

There were not too many regular tourists in the hotel; Managua did not have much to show except for poverty, misery, and destruction.

When the underground strengthened and became a full revolutionary movement, martial law was declared in the entire country. But the Sandinistas were not impressed; they pestered and attacked government buildings and officials, while their popular support increased. Gradually, most of the top military and political leaders started seeking refuge in the hotel after shipping their families away, mainly to Miami, the Latin American heaven.

The place became a wasp nest of feverish activities, rumors, meetings, hushed arrivals and departures, and armored vehicles parked in front. Spies, foreign officials, arms dealers, and generals wearing dark sunglasses crowded the hotel's public spaces, since there was practically no other place to confer or converse. In the lobby, one could hear the telex machine, the only civilian one in the country, which attracted a constant line of watchers hungry for news. Their hushed conversations were drowned out by its constant and loud clicking.

As the revolution turned into a full scale civil war, the hotel was abandoned by its staff, including the cooks, maids, and reception clerks. It was left in the hands of its guests who had the run of it.

This was the place where I made my new home.

Many evenings, sipping a drink or two at the hotel bar overlooking the ruins of the downtown, I listened to the lounge piano player. Like in the movie *Casablanca*, he was a permanent fixture in the hotel, and one of its nicest. He was from the Nicaragua Caribbean harbor town of Bluefields, an isolated settlement of former pirates and African slaves who spoke English as fluently as Spanish. I was one of his permanent audience members and he sometimes sat next to my table during his intermissions, accepting my offerings of a drink. This is how I learned about his origins, going back few centuries.

"I am a Garinagu, part of the Garifun community, a true Black Carib," he told me one evening. I waited till he finished his shift, invited him to a late bite, and persuaded him to explain the meaning of these words unheard before now. "We, the Garinagu people are few and spread among several Central American countries on the Caribbean Coast," he started telling the story of his people. "Our history began on a Caribbean island, way before it became a British colony. Indians of the Carib tribes in South America sailed in their wooded canoes to that island, where peaceful Arawak Indians lived. The Caribs killed their men and paired with the local women. What resulted was a language with a female Arawak version and a male Carib version, understood by both. A few generations later, two Spanish ships carrying African slaves sank close to the island. Some slaves survived, found shelter on the island, and mingled with the Arawak-Carib Indians. The fusion of people and races created the Garinagu people, the only free black people in the Caribbean who were never enslaved. Their cultures merged into a new one, Garifun.

The British colonizers, who settled the Caribbean islands and used black slaves on their plantations, did not tolerate a free black community. It was a bad example for other African slaves, not to be repeated. To solve this problem, the British Empire deported the entire Garinagu population to the remote Roatan Island, off the Honduran

Coast. Most of the deportees vanished during the relocation; the ones who survived were abandoned on the island with few supplies. However, instead of disappearing or diluting with other indigenous groups, the Garinagu survived as a distinctive black entity colonizing parts of the Caribbean Coast and becoming a thriving community with unique customs and music, of which I am a proud member," he finished.

When I asked him how big this community was, he gave me the number of 15,000-20,000 people, a vague estimate since nobody bothered to count them in their remote places of habitation.

Ironically, he was still remembering and singing, as part of his repertoire, an old song made famous in the U.S. by Carmen Miranda, at a time when Managua was a vibrant commercial and entertainment spot. Many times he had hotel guests telling him in a Humphrey Bogart fashion, "Play it again, Sam." Then he used to hit the piano keys obligingly and sing, accompanying himself:

Managua Nicaragua is a wonderful town
You buy a hacienda for few pesos down
You give it to the lady you are trying to win
But her papa doesn't let you come in

Managua Nicaragua what a wonderful spot
There is coffee and bananas and temperature hot…

Outside, the vast darkness of what used be downtown was punctured by small bonfires. They were among the roofless walls and ruins where people were still living, sleeping, cooking, loving, and hating, raising the new generation of Nicaragua in complete destitution and desperation.

Later, as I looked back, all was clear and obvious. But, at that time, I was almost oblivious to all the political commotion and unrest. I had never received any briefing from headquarters, and nobody else was there to give me a situation report to understand what was going on. I was just a young executive with a lot of money to blow away, making acquaintances and having a hell of a good time doing it. My naivety and lack of knowledge and understanding to what was going on around me was complete to the point where I seemed to disguise myself as an idiot among all the human sharks surrounding me.

When on a tour of duty in Central America, I used to spend a few days in Managua, and then I would catch a Pan American one-hour flight to El Salvador, spend a day there in meetings, catch another flight the next day to Guatemala City, and in the evening return back to my base, the hotel. Then I would do the south route, this time to San Juan in Costa Rica, then to Panama City, and back to my hole in the hotel. In Managua, my days started with a swim in the beautiful swimming pool surrounded by lush tropical vegetation, then sunbathing, some work, a lunch meeting, and a little siesta in the afternoon, ending the day with another business dinner. I liked the routine.

Not even my brief, but scary experience with a quake took this feeling away.

It was a Sunday afternoon, and I was in my room resting. Suddenly, my bed started shaking and moving. I felt like I was lying on the back of a galloping wild horse. The side lamps fell, shattering on the tile floor, the breaking noise telling me, beyond any doubt, what was happening. I rushed from my room down the stairs to the lobby. The stairs were littered with plaster and stucco fallen from the walls and ceilings. The elevators were out. The lobby was filled with shattered chandeliers, more debris, and chunks of fallen plaster. A bunch of scared guests were streaming down the stairs, rushing through the lobby, trying to get out of the building. However, no additional tremors followed, and shortly after, life resumed to its normal course, without any serious damages.

The hotel's design saved it once again. In the city, there was no excitement. Whatever could be affected by the quake had been destroyed already.

While staying in the hotel, my spending habits and the size of my business expense account attracted lots of guys and dolls seeking my company. Slowly, I started to realize I was surrounded either by professional people, experts in the trade of conspiracy and war, adventurers in search of thrills, or others looking for a free lunch.

There were few exceptions.

One of them was Lester Ross.

I met him accidentally one late evening in the hotel bar. After making the usual introductory small talk, he told me he was working for the World Bank, encouraging and financing projects in Central America. We were about the same age and our chemistry matched. A few drinks later, he made me feel comfortable to the point where I started to share with him details of my uneventful life. He kept encouraging me with additional cocktails, which freed my spirit and unleashed my tongue.

Our friendship grew even stronger after I bumped into him, accidentally, in the Sheraton of San Salvador, the capital of El Salvador, and a while later, in the Camino Real Hotel in Guatemala City. He was traveling the same route as me, meeting with potential borrowers in these countries. Our incidental encounters were funny; one Sunday morning while lunching in a luxurious, but remote hotel in Antigua, a picturesque little town in Guatemala, I accidentally turned my head around and who did I see having lunch next to me? Lester. Another time we bumped into each other on the same flight, from Managua to Panama City, and ended having a nice boys out night in that full of tempting opportunities city.

We went out in the evenings, had nice conversations, and I felt I had a friend in Central America. He had a great talent to get me talking, yet I could barely get anything out of him, including the projects he kept financing. He just explained, in general terms, the World Bank was actually a group of a few financial institutions set up by different governments after the end of the Second World War. Their purpose was to fight poverty by encouraging and financing large public projects in developing countries.

We also took weekend trips together. I remembered, even many years later, one of them when we drove north, from Managua to the picturesque mountain town of Matagalpa, then west to Leon, which was once the capital of the colonial Spanish Nicaragua. It was established by one of the great Spanish conquistadors, Hernandez de Cordoba. However, his popularity was disputed by a rival conquistador, the cruel Davila, who, as proof to his reputation, had Hernandez decapitated and put his head on display in the main city square. Now, more than

400 years later, the national currency of Nicaragua was called Cordoba, and the guy's head, the same one separated from its owner, was decorating all paper money bills. His image survived all political turmoil and many currency redesigns. Only the rapid inflation made these bills obsolete. Its beautiful cathedral became the symbol of the city and the Spanish heritage and even the match boxes had its picture.

We drove south, to the artisan markets of Masaya, where we saw endless displays of native art in colorful woven fabrics, straw and pottery. Its local artisan market was a magnet for the few tourists visiting the country, bringing some financial relief to its population. Some of these proceeds found their way to the political underground, bringing terrible consequences. The city, including its colorful stalls, was destroyed by the government tanks a year later while chasing the revolutionaries who took refuge there.

One incident increased my esteem of his personality and capabilities.

I just missed the only daily flight from Guatemala City to San Salvador, where I was supposed to meet a prospect for lunch and then catch the evening flight to Managua. Les and I had spent the night before in a drinking hole populated by locals only. It was not one of the places where you could find tourists. It was recommended by a local acquaintance who told us; to get the real spirit of Guatemala, we have to listen to a Marimba band. The joint was as unpretentious as any could be with some tables, chairs, a bar, and in the center, a marimba. It was a musical instrument I had never seen before. Like a large exposed piano, but longer, with wooden long tongues instead of cords in plain view. Five players stood next to each other, striking the wooden tongues with two sticks in each hand, mingling their hands together at dizzying speed and producing incredible melodious tunes, without any notes in front of them.

The following morning, my head foggy from the previous night's beers chased by some tequila shots, I was still going from one airline counter to another trying to find an alternate flight when I bumped into Lester. He was at the airport waiting for his flight back to Managua. Seeing my dilemma, he suggested we drive to San Salvador; I would meet my guy while he shopped for local curios in the artisans Mercado, then he would wait for me and we would return together in the evening to Managua. It sounded like a good idea, made easy by Lester who talked to one of the taxi drivers waiting in line outside the airport and agreed with him on a reasonable fee to drive us there.

We got into the back of the taxi, a big and old American sedan with a broken a/c. We rolled down the windows and relaxed on its torn seats while the driver took us on the Pan American Highway, connecting the two cities.

By early afternoon we were getting close to our destination, passing through one of the many sleepy villages and hamlets close to the two lane highway. Being siesta time, the whole settlement looked completely deserted. Few stray dogs were hiding from the scorching sun in the shadows of the huts, others moving around lazily.

Suddenly, a large man, stumbling drunk, came out of a shack by the side of the road and attempted to cross the highway ahead of our taxi. Before the driver could stop completely, the car hit the man, who landed with his face down on its large hood with a big thumping noise. He lay motionless and our driver was stunned. I opened the door trying to get out and help the poor man, if he was still alive, but Lester caught my arm and told me to sit and not move. Indeed, in less than a minute our taxi was surrounded by the entire hamlet, the men pacing vociferously around the taxi, while the women gathered together around a crying one, evidently the victim's better half.

Then the surrounding people moved away to give room to a man, the head of the hamlet, who gravely proceeded towards us.

Les motioned for him to get close to his open window and started a discussion in a rapid Spanish, accompanied by gesticulations and body language signs, which ended with a hand shake. Les, still sitting in same spot in the back seat, took out of his pocket a wad of quetzals, the Guatemalan currency, and passed it to the man. The alderman turned to the victim and told him few words with an authoritative voice. Immediately, the man came alive. He raised his head, listened to his leader, who had divided the money into two wads and was holding one in a hand stretched forward, sided off the taxi's hood, put the money in his pocket, and walked away, limping slightly, while the chief kept the other part.

In less than ten minutes from the beginning of the incident the road was deserted again, the victim walking away without any help. The dogs went back to their nap or search for food, while wondering about the commotion, so extraordinary for such a hot part of the day.

Our shaken driver delivered us at the door of the hotel in San Salvador. I kept my appointment at the scheduled time almost, while Les coolly proceeded to the lobby's bar and ordered himself a drink, waiting for me.

Meanwhile, the political situation became more perilous and the hotel, the only oasis of sanity and tranquility, became overcrowded. As an alternative, I started looking for a house to rent. To my surprise, in spite of the scarcity of decent housing in Managua, the local realtor found me a nice house in an exclusive and prestigious suburban neighborhood at a very attractively low rent.

I took it.

Only later did I understand why I lucked out.

It was a haunted house, at least in the eyes of the locals.

This house had been the scene of a very famous hostage situation and standoff event. A few years prior to my moving into the house it was considered one of the outstanding ones in Managua. It was a Spanish hacienda owned by a prominent socialite family, with five bedrooms and a beautiful large yard enclosed by a high stucco fence, in an elite area. The family and their house were well known for the social events sponsored there.

One of the events was the New Year's party.

That particular year, the hosts invited an array of guests: military, government officials, diplomats, and the social crème de la crème of the city. More than two hundred guests were crowded in the large patio and living room opening onto the yard, displaying the top fashion money could buy and jewelry that could light a few Christmas trees. As the evening progressed and the Nica Libre cocktails of rum and Coke started taking their toll, a few gun shots in the air shattered the party. A small group of young Sandinistas had broken into the house, barricaded themselves, and took everybody inside hostage. For two days the entire entourage stayed together, their makeup and clothing sticking to their sweaty bodies while the only food was the remains from the party. The resolution some of the lady guests made for the new coming year, to stop pigging out and lose some weight, was just about materializing.

The house was under siege.

Nobody left and nobody came in while the rebels waited for their demands, money and free passage. Many anecdotes and jokes were told about some of the guest ladies who preferred to swallow their jewels rather than surrendering them to the rebels. Finally, their demands were met and the siege was over without any casualties. Everybody was allowed to leave the house.

Since then nobody, the owners included, wanted to pass its threshold. The house was cleansed and the furniture was replaced, but it stood vacant till I, the clueless, rented it. This story did not bother me at all because it did not have a tragic ending. On the contrary, I found the jokes amusing about the guests and their emergency preservation of assets and, later on, about me, the sucker who was duped into renting the house. Besides, my use of the house was sporadic, a few days at a time with intervals in between.

The situation in the city became worse as time progressed, and shortly afterward, my local friends made me aware of the strictly enforced martial law imposed on the capital. A few times while coming from the airport, I found myself driving my rented car behind military open troop carriers, full of uptight soldiers in urban combat gear and holding rifles. Their white knuckled fingers were ready to press the trigger. In the hotel, guests were advised to limit their visits outside and never stay out late. Night curfews were imposed on the city, and the only traffic moving after 10:00 p.m. was the military patrols and vehicles displaying special travel permits and decals.

Of course, being in Managua, which, like the rest of Nicaragua, was nicknamed "The backyard of Somoza," one could always get a special traffic permit. It was given to all government officials and anybody who knew Somoza, or a general, or a relative of theirs. Then you could get a sticker affixed to your vehicle, allowing you to travel unrestricted and to be waved through roadblocks.

I was offered such a sticker and gladly accepted it.

It was the result of a dinner in a nice French restaurant, which was established in a private hacienda with very few tables and served excellent seafood and good booze. One of the rooms was transformed into a little gambling hall, a small casino with two blackjack tables and a small roulette wheel. I had invited a local client, a pillar of the community, to discuss business. Looking at my watch as the dinner lingered on I told my guest we needed to get back before curfew.

"Don't worry," he told me. "I have a permit and I'll take you back home. Leave your car here and tomorrow I'll get you a permit as well."

He seemed to be expecting somebody. Indeed, after a while, a young gentleman accompanied by two goons, guns sticking from underneath their shirts, walking respectfully behind him, entered the establishment and proceeded straight to one of the blackjack tables. All seats at the table were vacated instantly by the other players, after nodding with much respect and humility towards the newcomer. The dealer placed in front of him few stacks of tokens, most of them of high denomination. He started playing alone with the dealer, placing bets exceeding the maximum limits posted clearly on the table. The dealer did not object. My guest for dinner left his seat and approached the guy with a slight bow and said few words of pleasantries accompanied by humble gestures. The gambler barely acknowledged his presence with a slight nod of his head and turned his attention back to the cards on the table. My guest came back to our table and sat down with a look of satisfaction. Seeing the question marks in my eyes, he motioned me to wait. After less than half an hour the young gentleman got up briskly from the blackjack table and, without a word, left the place together with his entourage. My guest accompanied the leaving party with his eyes in hope for another sign of recognition. When they were out, he turned to me and said, bending secretively, as about revealing something of importance; "Don't you know who this person is?" Seeing the lack of recognition reflected in my looks he added; "He is President Somoza's son, our next President, maybe. I knew he might be coming here and I am so happy he saw me. It means a lot to me and to my business."

"How did you know he might come here?" I asked.

He answered with a twinkle of humor in his eyes, his face flushed by the imbibed alcohol;" He is a gambler, but of a special kind. When he wins he pockets his winnings. When he loses he does not pay. The owners of the place have to put up with this, otherwise their little casino would be shut overnight."

The restaurant tab that night was extravagant—my guest showing an unsatisfying thirst for after dinner drinks. It was the reward he felt entitled to, although his metabolism objected and punished him with a severe case of drunkenness.

The next day I had a special travel permit sticker affixed to my rental, while its donor was still in bed, unable to get rid of his hangover.

Events started to unfold faster in the last week I spent in Managua, just before it was taken over by the Sandinistas and Somoza fled the country.

Not that it helped him a lot. Somoza hoped to reach safer grounds in Paraguay, a notoriously lawless country with wide limits of patience for fallen-from-grace political dictators, as well as a haven for Nazis and Fascists who found shelter and cover from the long arms of the International Tribunals for War Crimes. It did not take too long before he was blown to pieces, in his armored limousine, in the center of Asuncion, the capital city. His dispatch to eternity was carried out by a group of paramilitary using shoulder bazookas. One of them was a direct hit and Somoza's car disintegrated, sending him to heaven with a lot of lights and sound effects he had loved so much.

It was later speculated that the liquidators were sent by Castro. Others claimed it was an act of revenge of a personal nature. The local affluent German community in Paraguay, reinforced by newly arrived Nazis fleeing justice in Europe, avenged the German minority in Nicaragua. Much of Somoza's family fortunes originated from assets Somoza, the father, had confiscated, with the silent approval of his American benefactors, from the German colony in Nicaragua at the end of the Second World War.

Payback day had finally arrived in the true Biblical way; sons had to pay for their father's sins.

The week started with a beautiful, cloudless Sunday morning in Managua.

My car had quit on me the day before, and I was waiting for the rental company to replace it as soon as somebody else returned a rental. The company just did not have many cars, and it was the only one left operating in the entire country.

I was bored.

I tried to get a hold of Les at the hotel, but he was no where to be found. Next I called one of my local friends, Jorge, who was a constant source of entertainment ideas.

He was the one who had also given me an eye opening crash course in local economics. Visiting one of his business ventures, a garment assembly plant, I noticed a long line of people snaking patiently in front of his gated plant. Seeing the question in my eyes, he told me; "Look at them. This is their only hope. The line forms day after day and it starts before dawn. These people come uninvited, hoping and ready to get any job offered, making in a day much less than one hour of minimum wage in the States. If they get hired, they don't feel exploited or underpaid. On the contrary, it is a fortunate event. The only other choice is to have nothing, including food."

I was looking at them and at my friend. From one side, a bunch of skinny, poorly dressed worried people. Facing them was Jorge, balding but with a pony tail of whatever hair was left, sporting a beer belly, dressed in a nice shirt with short sleeves and a tie, to show everybody who the boss is, his shirt already stained with dark sweat spots .

The plant was an illustration of local businesses. It consisted of a trailer used as the main offices and a large enclosed shack used as a raw materials and finished goods warehouse, each of the structures located at opposite sides of a large fenced yard. The yard itself was the assembly plant. Dozens of industrial sewing machines were lined on the bare ground, one behind the other, separated by the twisting, above- ground electrical wires powering them, and were operated by women and men bent over them laboriously, especially when one of the supervisors was passing by. While visiting this sweatshop, we were standing in the middle of the yard under a tree, and Jorge's little daughter was playing next to him with a little doll. Suddenly, in a whirl of motion, a small monkey jumped from the tree, grabbed the doll from the girl's hands, climbed back up a branch, and started grooming the doll like a mother grooms a baby. Nothing, not even a banana, could persuade the monkey to return the doll, and the girl left without it.

That day he was busy with a family affair. Sunday in Nicaragua, as in all of Central America, was a day do dedicate to the church and to the family. However, he suggested I try a beautiful remote beach on the Pacific coast, San Juan Del Sur, about 100 kilometers south of the city, close to the border of Costa Rica. I told him I didn't have a car, and an hour later, his younger brother showed up with a car for me to use. It was a nice Alfa Romeo sedan and its looks motivated me to give it a try. After I drove the brother back, I continued driving south and two hours later I was there.

Just before the road ended, in front of the sandy beach, an enormous billboard was planted so everybody could see it. It was a big hand painted portrait of President Somoza sitting relaxed in a comfortable chair, dressed in a black suit, white shirt and red tie, his eyes framed by heavy rimmed glasses looking with fatherly benevolence at his flock. Two big words accompanied the picture; 'Somoza! Forever!' Coming from the city about to collapse into the hands of his enemies, I smiled at the irony of these two words.

It was indeed a beautiful beach, and, being Sunday, it was full of lots of colorful, happy locals. It was peaceful and relaxing, in complete contrast to the gloomy spirits in the capital city.

I rented a little palm hut on the beach, passing as a cabana. In the heat of the afternoon and with help from the monotonous noise of the rolling waves, I took a nap on the slowly moving hammock.

By the time I woke up and finished a simple, but delicious seafood dinner, prepared in front of my eyes at one of the fishermen stands, the sun started setting. Its hazy bottom touched the endless Pacific and then started sinking into the ocean.

I got into the car and headed back to Managua.

A dirt road climbed away from the beach, leading to the Pan-American Highway. It was named in that part Carretera del Sur, a two-lane road connecting Managua with the main cities along the Pacific coast.

I missed a turn and by the time I found my way back, it was completely dark.

The darkness slowed my driving.

The highway passed through little villages and hamlets, and I was busy overtaking horses and oxen-pulled carts, the main transportation in that area. Every few minutes I had to squeeze my car between crowded, small, smoky, Japanese made minivans used as public transportation, dropping and picking passengers, some of them hanging by the sides of the open doors. Some of these hamlets did not even have electricity; and I drove through them at a crawling pace to avoid hitting the children playing and people chatting by the sides of the road, the only lights coming from kerosene lamps in the shacks close by.

I was getting close to Managua when I noticed a few cars coming from the opposite direction flashing their headlights at me. The reason became clear shortly after—a roadblock.

The dark road unveiled it a short distance ahead, masked by the darkness and by the fatigue uniforms of the three soldiers manning it. As I stopped before the barrels blocking half the road, two of the soldiers stood up lazily and proceeded to my car, one on each side.

I looked at the windshield and I realized, with horror, it did not have a visible permit sticker. The soldier on my side motioned for me to lower my window.

"Papeles de viaje, por favor (travel documents, please)," he said, noticing the absence of the sticker.

I turned on the interior lights, bent to the passenger side and opened the glove compartment under the scrutinizing eyes of both soldiers. There were no documents in it. Its space was taken up by a shining black gun and two ammo clips. I stopped breathing for a long moment, my hand stopped in mid-air. I knew having any firearm in a vehicle was strictly prohibited. Under the martial law, no civilian, under any circumstances, was entitled to possess, or, worse, to carry firearms. Before I could close the glove compartment my slight hesitation was noticed and, with surprising speed, both doors were opened at the same time.

I was pulled out by one soldier, while the second bent inside the car, grabbed the gun and the clips and joined his colleague in holding me.

Attracted by the unfolding sequence, the third soldier approached the car. He was clearly the higher ranking. He came towards me slowly, sizing me up and down and then circling around. Reaching my back, he stopped and moments later I felt handcuffs around my wrists. For the first and the only time in my life I felt the metal touch of the cuffs on my wrist bones, and the feeling is still engraved in my memory.

Then, without any hurry, he stuck his head inside the car. He found my backpack with the stuff I took to the beach and not finding in it anything of interest, took the keys from the ignition, went to the back of the car, and opened the trunk.

I was watching him, seeing only part of his bent body. After some time, which seemed like an eternity, he straightened and emerged from under the trunk lid.

Surprise, surprise.

He was holding a big machete in its leather sheath, a large sword-like knife used widely by the locals for cutting anything in the fields and in the jungle. People in Central America have been known to use machetes to cut enemies as well. It was considered the most useful and efficient weapon of choice locally. It was the first time I saw it, having no reason to open the trunk, but nobody was there to ask or to listen to me.

The searcher motioned with his head to the soldiers holding me, and they dragged me away from the side of the road and from the light coming out of my car's headlights, still turned on, giving the scene a surrealistic feel.

Nobody talked.

Reaching a grassy spot close to the bench used by the soldiers, the same soldier planted himself in front and proceeded to unceremoniously search my pockets. The only identification with me was my international driving license and a few of my business cards. My passport was locked in a safe in the house. However, I had on me a considerable amount of money, the equivalent of a few months of average military pay. I became used to carrying money, in local and U.S. dollars. In most of the local establishments, credit cards were not accepted and "dinero" replaced the "Diners Club" card in my wallet. The searcher stopped. Holding my possessions and giving a short order to one of the soldiers, he turned around and went back to the roadblock, waving through the few cars that had meanwhile stopped at the barricaded road. He was in a hurry and did not even bother to pretend he was checking travel permits. Within a few seconds, the road became deserted again.

The two soldiers next to me exchanged glances, and then it dawned on me, I was about to be robbed, if not worse. For the first time since I was stopped I felt real fear creeping through my entire body, like a splash of iced water. They dragged me further into the darkness and threw me on the ground. I fell on my back, my hands still cuffed behind. A booted leg inserted behind rolled me over with my face in the grass. I felt hands removing the watch from my left wrist; I did not have any other ornaments—no rings, necklaces, or bracelets. Then I heard their voices discussing, from what I understood, how to dispose of me.

The unit leader made a decision. He shouted to the soldier at the barricade to keep waving vehicles through and, together with the other, dragged me on the grass further away from the road toward some bushes. A debate followed; to shoot me with the gun they found on me or to use the machete.

"Use the machete," he ordered the soldier. "We don't need the noise."

I could not see anything, my head being stuck deep in the grass. I knew I was just about to expire, and the only thought going through my mind was how my messy body would look when found.

No blow ever came.

Instead, a sudden cry of surprise, and it didn't come from me. I heard muffled noises, two puffs and the acrid smell of gunpowder filled my nostrils. T hen, complete silence, broken only by the loud courting noises of the cicadas.

A soundless pair of Nike shoes approached my field of vision, and then somebody bent over my back, inserted a key, and released my handcuffs. I turned my face up.

Lester towered above me as he got back on his feet.

He motioned with a finger on his lips to keep quiet and, after helping me to get up, pushed me in front of him toward a car parked on the other side of the roadblock hidden by bushes, its front doors open and the interior lights off. As I got in, Les darted back into the darkness with astonishing agility. I watched his shadow as it got closer to the remaining soldier. With a quick, small flash of light accompanied by another subdued puff, the soldier's body crumpled and fell on the road. Les pulled him quickly into the bushes, returned to the barricade barrels, and moved them away, into the darkness.

What was a military roadblock a short while ago became another undisturbed part of the deserted road.

We left behind three bodies; the following day's headlines announced that, in an escalation of hostilities, the Sandinistas attacked a roadblock and killed three soldiers, one of them a captain.

In the car I started to shake, getting into a post traumatic state of shock. Les pulled from under his seat a bottle of Flora de Cana—the excellent local rum—took a long sip, and offered it to me. A few mouthfuls later, I started to calm down. Meanwhile, Les was waiting patiently, without any display of emotion, for me to come back to my senses. He was a person completely different from the one I knew, one I never saw before—controlled, calculated, self confidence emanating from him.

In a soft voice he said; "We have to act fast before your car is discovered. You'll have to get over there and drive your car away."

I followed his instructions and returned to my car. But, trying to start it, I remembered the searching soldier took the keys. I told Les and he disappeared back into the darkness. When he emerged, he was carrying the keys, my documents, the cash, the watch, and the machete. He was limping.

"What happened?" I asked him.

"One of the soldiers was still alive and tried to sharpen the machete on my leg," he answered smiling, but with a grimace of pain. "I guess by now he joined his colleagues in hell. This time I made sure he was heading that way."

In the darkness I noticed the lower part of his pants was slashed, and around the rip, a dark shadow of blood was expanding slowly. I proceeded to remove part of the cut fabric, twisted it till it became an improvised rope and tied it tightly around the wound as a tourniquet, stopping the bleeding. An argument followed as I tried to convince Les to be a passenger in my car and let me drive him to a hospital.

I lost, he won. It was too dangerous to leave any vehicle close by and to show up in a hospital, with three military corpses lying by the side of the road waiting to be discovered. He sat with difficulty in his car, and both of us proceeded to drive, in separate vehicles, away from the scene.

An hour later we arrived to my house. He parked his car behind mine and both got out at the same time. He went to the back of his car, took the jack from its trunk and, with a swift motion, smashed the passenger side window of the Alfa Romeo I drove. Then, he went to the trunk and forced it open, breaking its lock. Turning to me, he said; "When you return the car to your friend, tell him it was broken in while you were taking a nap on the beach. This way you'll avoid unnecessary questions about the whereabouts of the gun and the machete."

He went back to his car, sat down with difficulty while trying to find a comfortable position for his wounded leg, called me to his rolled down window and said; "I know you need some explanations, but let's leave them for tomorrow. Just keep in mind that I did what had to be done to save your life and to make sure nobody would be left to connect you with what happened."

Then he sped away.

After he left I found myself sitting alone in the living room staring blankly at the bare walls, with a complete void in my mind. I kept taking one sip after another from the rum bottle Les had pushed into my hands before driving away. Finally, they started to work on my system and I fell asleep fully dressed, still covered with dirt and grass.

The following day we met early in the morning.

It was in the main hospital in Managua where Les had checked himself in after leaving me and realizing his bleeding was still there, accompanied by sharp pains. The adrenalin had stopped flowing and pain killers were needed to replace it. When asked, Les told the admitting nurse he was mugged at knife point and tried to be brave, his courage being compensated by the deep cut in his lower left leg just below the knee. Meanwhile, the wound had swollen and the redness of infection started to spread. He was admitted immediately for a deep scrub of the wound, stitches, and intravenous antibiotic infusion. Before being transferred from the admission room into the treatment area, Les, as a foreigner, was given the special privilege of using the nurse's phone to call the hotel and leave a message with the receptionist concerning his whereabouts. This is how I found out where he was.

The public hospital was located not far away from the hotel, but a world apart. It was a compound of a few barracks, almost like a military camp, the white paint turning to dirty gray wherever it had not peeled yet. They were located in a large field littered with garbage, overgrown by wild grass and brush, surrounded by a barbed wire fence. The entrance was guarded by a soldier who needed to know what brought a person there; he was also the final judge to decide who gets in and who stays out. No other triage was needed. A large number of people, some of them visitors and some needing medical attention, were waiting patiently, standing or squatting, for a change of mood or a change of guards. Being dressed, acting, and talking like a Gringo, I was let in without any hassle. As I entered inside the perimeter I could see, on the grounds leading to the admission entrance, dark spots of what could only be blood.

Inside, the patients were treated in large dormitories containing twelve beds each, all of them occupied. Some were pacing slowly among the beds pushing the rolling stands with intravenous fluids ahead of them, other moaning from pains, some laying without moving. The tiled floor was dirty and the air was filled with cigarettes smoke while a ceiling ventilator was trying desperately to bring in some fresh air through the open windows. A single, mature nurse, in nuns uniform, was attempting to attend the needs of all the suffering, moving silently among the beds with a permanent smile of kindness and listening with infinite patience to the complaints coming from everybody.

I found Les and pulled up a chair next to him, only after his signal that he wished to talk to me. I knew that our subject of conversation would not be the weather report, so I got as close as I could to him.

Pale from loss of blood and, evidently, in lots of pain, he was stretched on the hospital bed, one leg lifted and heavily bandaged.

Without fanfare, Les started talking right away, before I even had a chance to ask anything; "Robert, there are few things I wish to tell you. My name is Lester, but everything else you know about me is not accurate. Actually, I don't even work for the World Bank. I work for the U.S. Government."

Noticing the stupefaction in my eyes, he said with a contemptuous voice; "Wake up, man. Stop being a child. This is a very rough part of the world. You should have known by now. Yes, I work for The Company. Yes, the C.I.A."

Then he started to unravel the truth, parts of which would be challenged many years later.

My business activities, meetings, travel, and spending attracted a lot of attention unbeknownst to me. One particular dinner, which continued with after drinks and discussions late into the night with a new acquaintance I had made in the hotel, rang alarm bells. Not knowing, I kept company with a retired Israeli general who had become an international arms supplier and, as a result, was a person of interest to several governments. He was under surveillance, and our dinner together lit a spotlight over my head. Les was assigned, as a field agent for the C.I.A., to find out if I was involved in any arms transactions or if I was a foreign agent. At the beginning, Les believed I was connected to the Mossad, the Israeli intelligence agency, which was quite active in that part of the world. My business activities and naïve behavior were considered a facade, in the beginning. Only our consequent encounters convinced him I was as clueless and ignorant as I looked, and I had no idea about what was happening around me. However, his assignment was to follow me wherever I went, especially after noticing I had become the center of interest for two more intelligence agencies, a result of my social encounters. Moreover, he was put in charge of my well being and protecting me while in Central America.

This revelation sounded flattering, a compliment to my soaring ego—I was Robert...the spy.

I liked it.

When asked about our accidental meetings in other parts of Central America, he smiled and answered; "There are no coincidences in our line of business, and no accidental encounter is accidental. Robert, remember this axiom and you'll save yourself from a lot of trouble in the future."

That Sunday, when I borrowed the Alfa Romeo, he had followed me to the beach.

Actually, he liked the tranquility of that beach so much, he promised himself to come back one day, maybe for a longer period of time. He had the same relaxing time I had, except for the nap he never took. He followed my car back to Managua; he saw it being stopped and driven slowly through the roadblock, and he saw me handcuffed on the side of the road. It was clear to him what was happening. He realized that it was either me or the three soldiers. Having made the determination quickly, he used the surprise factor and overcame the two soldiers next to me with much ease. He was neither expected nor detected, and before they could react, they were gone.

As I listened to him, the pieces started falling into place and created, like a solved puzzle, a clear picture.

Before leaving him, Les added; "Robert, it is time for you to leave this country and go home. This place is just about exploding and there is no reason whatsoever for you to be here. Let's hope we'll meet in some better place in the future. Hey, who knows, maybe on that nice beach?"

In spite of his warning, I came back that afternoon and for the next three days, as long as Les stayed in the hospital. Three days of constant nursing, attending, and offering my undivided time and attention. It was necessary; private nurses or individual care were not words to be found in the local medical lexicon. Obviously I felt guilty, the wound being caused by my carelessness. In addition, my feelings of friendship, which seemed to be mutual, were strong enough to make any efforts to improve his situation. Less tried to put me at ease; repeating time after time that danger came with the territory in his profession. Finally, the day arrived when he could walk, limping.

I released him from the hospital, the medical bill being taken care of by his employer. After another day of recovering in his hotel room, Les was driven to the airport by his freshly arrived replacement.

Two days later I packed my belongings, closed the house, and left Nicaragua on one of the last flights aboard Lanica, its national airline, before it was taken away from its owner, Anastasio Somoza.

When I met Lester again, many years later, it was, of course, not by accident.

Les had taught me not to believe in coincidences and accidental meetings.

By then I was an importer of automotive parts or, as my friends used to call me, an international businessman. One of my trips brought me to Washington, D.C.

I landed late morning and proceeded to the luggage carousel. Concentrating on the swirl of identical luggage while trying to identify my own, I did not pay attention to the surrounding people, and I did not notice the person approaching me.

There was a slight tap on my shoulder, and I turned around to see Lester.

He had no luggage in his hands except for a long, rectangular carton, the same kind florists used for Mother's Day shipments of roses. We hugged, patting each other's shoulders, and our eyes took inventory. Some changes were noticeable; few additional pounds around the waist, his hair thinner and graying around the temples, and a slight limp.

Observing the silent question in my eyes, Les said jokingly; "This is a present from you."

Later, after I collected my luggage, we found a quiet spot in one of the airport bars. There were only a few customers, all caught up in a soundless sports event on TV. Even the metallic voice over the system, announcing arrivals and departures, was muted and we could conduct a conversation.

The limp was a result of the machete slash in Nicaragua, Lester told me.

By the time he reached decent medical facilities, the wound had once again become a large red, swollen spot spreading to most of his leg. The medical staff could not decide if it was a case of blood poisoning or tetanus. They did agree, however, as his temperature kept escalating, that his life was in danger. The only possible hope was to amputate. For few days he soaked the sheets with disease induced sweat, drifting in and out consciousness. Then his temperature started going down. As the attending doctors were still debating next to him, he got out of bed without any help and went to the bathroom.

The disease was over. However, the surgeons had removed part of the infected leg muscle and the limp would remain forever.

After recuperating, Les was sent back to Central America, this time on a planning and coordination assignment.

Meanwhile, the Sandinistas had won the civil war in Nicaragua and the newly formed government was not sympathetic to the Americans. It made many politicians unhappy and calls for action were made. The Agency established a new command post in Tegucigalpa, the capital of neighboring Honduras. From there, subversive and covert activities were planned and conducted. Their purpose was to weaken the Cuban influenced Sandinista government and help build an underground movement in Nicaragua.

The cold war moved close to American shores and the Agency started the same warfare strategy used to combat communism in Europe.

Lester became instrumental in planning the logistics of these operations. This was how he met a young and ambitious colonel who kept shuttling between D.C. and Honduras, flying a fighter jet assigned to him by the Pentagon. Coordinating the secret activities of supporting and financing these covert activities, this officer became the central person in the Central American exploits underwritten by the U.S. Lester became his field assistant.

Those were tough days for C.I.A. Congressional scrutiny, media exposure and an Administration weary to assist the ill-reputed Agency left its secret fund coffers almost empty. No official budget was allocated to assist and equip the Nicaraguan underground. Vast amounts were needed by these freedom fighters, called "contras," and they were looking with expectations at their supporters in D.C.

Then with a flash of perverse brilliancy, a secret plan was developed. Through middlemen and third parties, negotiations were conducted with Middle Eastern countries, which were on the Department of State list of terrorist countries. They were holding American hostages. As the plan went, the Pentagon sold these countries a variety of weaponry requested by them. Against each shipment of weapons, hostages were to be released. In addition, these new clients, mainly Iran—which had changed its name to the Islamic Republic of Iran—paid enormous amounts of money for the shipments. The Pentagon received only a small part. Another part went into the pockets of the middlemen.

The remainder, a large one, went to a secret fund created to assist the contras and finance the C.I.A. war in Central America.

The plan, which was discovered and exposed by the media, became famous in the States as the "arms for hostages" and "the contras affair." The main issue was the illegality of supplying weapons to terrorist countries. It also contradicted the stated Presidential policy of not negotiating with terrorists. Administration officials, including the President, denied, lied, and when all excuses were exhausted, found the fall guys. One of them was the young colonel who had been in the center of these international conspiracies. His fall from grace left Lester without any immediate supervisor in charge of Central America operations, and by the virtue of being there and next in line, he became "our man in Honduras."

He was there when a plane chartered by C.I.A., full with weapons to the contras, was downed by a young Nicaraguan soldier, triggering an international media storm. It was proof beyond any doubt of the C.I.A. being the supplier of weapons to the contras, in an attempt to topple the legally, democratically elected Nicaraguan government.

He was on the spot when the funds started drying out, while the public opinion became more and more venomous towards the C.I.A. intervention in Central America. By then, the underground activities had spread to Costa Rica and El Salvador, a country devastated by a civil war born from the ashes of the contras.

Lester spent a few tumultuous years in this labyrinth of subversive activities, contras training camps, and pipelines of tactical supplies. The few C.I.A. officers still involved, high in its hierarchy, were impressed by his performance under duress and his loyalty to the cause of the Agency.

Then the end of the cold war, the end of the underground in Nicaragua, and even the end of the civil war in El Salvador left only Guatemala in turmoil, but the military junta was strong enough to not need American assistance. Lester was reclaimed to Langley and offered a position of utmost secrecy and importance—to help plan the future of the Agency.

After finishing his introduction, Lester bent forward looking at me and said; "Robert, I am here on a mission."

"What is it?" I asked.

"I want you," he answered. "I would like to see you join our team at the Agency. We need people like you"

"Why me?" I asked, looking at him with complete surprise.

Could he know my secret, only known to a handful of people in the entire world?

"Robert, you belong with us, you are part of the family," he kept pressing.

"What did I do to deserve this honor? What are you talking about?" I asked, trying to keep my composure.

Les looked at me for a long moment, straightened himself in his seat, and looking straight into my eyes, said; "I am going to tell you a long story and then you decide, okay?"

I made a phone call to postpone my scheduled meetings for the day, turned my cell phone off, and told Lester; "I am all ears. Go ahead."

Lester got up, went to the bar counter, and came back with two beers, gave one and said; "You might need a drink. Just sit tight and listen."

He installed himself in the chair, finding a comfortable position for his stiff leg, and started telling the story of a missing part in my life…

"For many years I kept asking myself and others what was behind the special treatment and opportunities given to you, Robert, by your employer, especially in Central America. I tried to get it from you as well, but it became clear you had no idea. Moreover, you didn't even know you had a bodyguard, I, in charge of your wellbeing while in Nicaragua. My assignment was basically to watch over you and get you out of trouble. The story I remember telling as the reason for being around you was an excuse. Indeed, the friends you had made there attracted undesirable attention, but we knew who you were." He stopped for a moment and then asked; "Tell me, Robert, hadn't you suspected I was there for you all the time?"

"How can I ever forget that you saved my life?" I answered.

"But Robert, there were other instances when I saved your skin and you were not aware of the dangerous situations you were in. Even now, many years later, I remember how your ignorance almost got you in a Nicaraguan military jail. You probably don't even know what I am talking about." Seeing my puzzled look, he asked; "Do you remember your French Foreign Legion hat?"

Actually, I vaguely remembered something about a hat being taken away from me by customs in Managua. A hat I had bought in a flea market in Marseilles, the headquarters of the French Foreign Legion. Designed for the heat of Sahara, it was perfect for the merciless sun in Central America.

Wanting to make sure, I asked him; "What are you talking about?"

"The French Legion hat you had on your head when you landed in Managua. You wore a military hat, part of a military combat uniform, which was strictly forbidden because the rebels wore similar ones. You probably forgot, but you were taken to a detaining room at the airport, on the way to being dispatched to a military holding pen for political prisoners. I remember clearly your surprise; I was just behind you and watching. You didn't realize your military hat was like a red flag in front of a furious bull. You kept arguing, refusing to remove and surrender it to the enraged customs guy. I had to make quite a few calls to be able to get you out of trouble, and you never suspected your behind was about to be kicked big time. Actually, you came out of that room still complaining that your hat was confiscated, oblivious to the trouble it brought on you."

I nodded silently. Memories came back and knowing what I learned later, the story made sense.

Looking at me, Les said; "Let's get back to the main subject, your preferential treatment. The answer was revealed many years later."

He stopped for a moment and then continued;

"With the fall of the Berlin Wall and the fast turn of events which eliminated the communist systems in Eastern Europe, many of The Fronts, the dummy corporations created by C.I.A. overseas to facilitate its subversive and underground activities, were dismantled or transferred into private hands. The enemy was gone and they were no longer needed.

One of these corporations was the one which employed you and sent you over to Central America. It had been used, while it existed, as a conduit of money and other resources to underground movements battling the communism in Europe, this being the reason for the location of its headquarters. Its wealth derived from the deep coffers of the Agency more than from the usual course of business. Funny enough, later it became quite a profitable entity, generating profits and additional funds for the Company. You, without knowing, were serving the same employer as me, Uncle Sam and the Company, doing some legwork and gathering basic background information.

When this particular façade became history, not being needed anymore, it was sold and its files were transferred to Langley, Virginia, to the main archive.

At that point in time, I was already in my new basement office in Langley, being initiated into the intricate relationships within the Agency, as well as its relations with the Pentagon and F.B.I. As a part of this education, I was given almost unlimited access to the Company's archives. Learning its history was an integral part of being able to plan the future. This is where I found your file, with the scribbling of your bosses and your history, going back one generation, to your father.

The story starts before you were born, just after the end of the Second World War, on another continent, in another country—Romania."

"Why Romania?" I asked Les.

"Because this is where you were born," he answered, observing my reaction.

I knew this fact already, although it was a recent and most surprising revelation. However, not to disappoint Les, my savior and role model, I pretended to be taken by complete surprise and encouraged him to continue. He did;

"Robert, I know this comes as a complete shock and surprise and you probably don't have any ideas about this country and how it relates to events in your life. Let me take the liberty and give you some background; it will help you understand how and why we met, way back in Nicaragua."

I nodded in agreement and he continued;

"Romania, like many other countries in Europe, was a combination of a few distinct ethnical and geographical parts, which were annexed, taken away, and annexed again during its modern history as a nation, from the middle of the nineteenth century to the mid twentieth century. These political allegiances and separations created ethnical and national minorities, the most evident being the Jewish population as well as the Hungarian, Russian, German, and Bulgarian nationalities. In addition, the Roma nation, better known as gypsies, found temporary residence in Romania. Incidentally, there is no relation between the names Romania and Roma; the similarity is strictly coincidental.

The Romanians, believing very much like the Germans in national purity, were not delighted with the infusion of minorities. Feelings were amplified when, given the chance, a large part of them migrated to Bucharest, the capital, and attempted to assimilate.

Bucharest was a unique city of lights, joie-de-vivre, and cultural enlightenment. Embracing the French culture, it was nicknamed 'The Little Paris,' with a touch of Latin spirit. Even the Romanian language, although spiced with many words and expressions borrowed from French, has been rooted in Latin, an inheritance left by the Roman settlers. Belonging, in the distant past, to the outer limits of the Roman Empire, the heritage was cherished and set it apart from its Slavic and Turco-Hungarian neighbors.

The architecture was reminiscent of Paris, with the same imposing residential buildings, large boulevards, and even an Arch of Triumph. As in Paris, 'Arcul de Triumf' is in the middle of an enormous traffic circle, and from it, main boulevards spread in all directions, like the spokes of a gigantic wheel.

By the way, Robert, most of these buildings don't exist anymore.

They were erased by an earthquake and whatever remained intact was taken down by its infamous dictator, Ceausescu. He erected a presidential palace with more than 9,000 rooms, spreading throughout entire neighborhoods that had to be erased to the ground.

Embracing Western Civilization, Romanians turned their back to the East. The mingling minorities arriving to the city from eastern territories were discriminated against, especially the Jewish community.

A strong anti-Semitic political movement started developing in Romania. Its followers were called 'legionnaires,' members of the 'Legion of the Archangel Michael.' The movement evolved into a powerful political party, unique in modern European history. It was a party based on religion, the Romanian-Orthodox Church, but supported by a paramilitary arm, "the Iron Guard."

In spite of Romania being a monarchy, the king himself being blood related to the British royal family, its political system was based on a parliamentary coalition. In this power sharing system, the legionnaires and the Iron Guard flourished and became an integral part. It led to strengthening of the anti-Semitism, in parallel to Nazi Germany."

"So, if the King was related to the British monarchy, I assume he opposed the Nazis and whatever they stood for," I ventured to interject.

Les answered; "When the Second World War started, Romania tried to take a neutral stand. However, after the fall of Poland and Czechoslovakia, the political leaders came to the sad conclusion that France and Great Britain, traditionally the fall-back, could not be relied upon anymore. So, to save the country from a similar fate, they joined Germany, as one of its Axis members. Its troops became part of the German war effort against the Soviet Union. It was an alliance of convenience. Germany offered protection from the Russian Army and Romania offered vast natural resources, especially oil and soldiers to fight the Red Army.

This is the period when the Iron Guard, reinforced by German presence, reached a new high level of political power and clout, accompanied by intense anti-Semitic actions. Jewish property was confiscated without any proceedings, Jewish professionals were barred from daily activities, and the media was constantly reminding the population of its duty to eradicate any Jewish influence. Looting was a daily occurrence in Bucharest and violence replaced the rhetoric."

"No casualties?" I asked.

Les answered;" In 1941, a wild massacre of the Jewish population took place in this emancipated and culturally advanced city. The Iron Guard, leading a mob, attacked Jewish neighborhoods, burning homes, synagogues, and Jewish community centers and killing, raping, and torturing hundreds of innocent civilians. It was the worst pogrom ever to take place in a major European city. The cruelty exceeded even the worst nightmares; it culminated with the cry, 'La abator cu jidani,' meaning, 'let's take the Jews to the slaughterhouse.' Dozens of Jewish men, women, and children were dragged from their homes and taken to the local slaughterhouse. There they were tortured, murdered, and their mutilated bodies were hung on cattle hooks like slaughtered animals. The participating crowds cheered the sights, attaching anti-Semitic slur to the hanging bodies, which were left for days on the slaughterhouse hooks.

The massacre created political repercussions for the Iron Guard and the legionnaires. Even the Germans condemned their actions; they believed in systematic extermination of Jews, not wild and uncontrolled displays of savagery. The Romanian Prime Minister, General Antonescu, was infuriated. He was not less anti-Semitic; however, the Iron Guard competed with the official government in looting and confiscating Jewish property. Antonescu wanted these assets for himself and for the Romanian war effort against the Russians. In addition, the Iron Guard killed some of the Romanian military for their refusal to participate in the massacre.

After a quick, but determined, massive military action against the Iron Guard militia, it was outlawed and excommunicated from any political life in Romania."

"So, the Romanian government was not so bad to the Jewish population, after all," I interrupted Les.

"Ha, you really make me laugh. Just listen to what happened afterwards," Les said.

"Antonescu was indeed accused and labeled as a 'Jew lover,' and his political enemies used his objection to the Iron Guards and the fact that both his stepmother and his first wife were Jewish as evidence against him. But his Anti-Semitic position was clarified beyond any doubt by two events.

Shortly after his power became unchallenged, Antonescu ordered his military governor in the northern city of Iasi to eliminate its Jewish population. In the days following this order, more than 15,000 Jewish men, women, and children were taken out of their homes, rounded, and killed. Some were shot in the streets, which became blood baths, their bodies left to be buried by surviving victims or left to rot in plain view.

Others were loaded onto cattle trains, which moved at a snail's pace between Romanian towns and villages waiting for the unfortunate passengers to die from exposure, thirst, and hunger. It was the Romanian version of extermination camps.

The Jewish people were also lined up in the main local train station and ordered to lie on the floor, forming a human carpet. Soldiers descending from trains arriving with military reinforcements stepped on this living and breathing floor, crushing skulls and bodies with their boots. Whoever survived these atrocities were sent to labor camps in Russian annexed territories, primarily Transnistria. The Romanian population scavenged whatever the soldiers and their accompanying teams of looters left behind after robbing, ransacking, and burning the Jewish homes of Iasi.

The second incident took place a short time later. The Romanian army, as part of the German attack forces, defeated the Red Army and conquered the Russian city of Odessa. This city had been a center of cultural and commercial Jewish activity, with a large Jewish population. After the Red Army retreated, local Russian partisans blew up the Romanian occupation headquarters in the city. When informed about the Romanian military casualties, who included a few officers, Antonescu gave a harsh order to take revenge on the Jewish population. A multitude of pogroms in Odessa and neighboring towns resulted. When it was over, more than 300,000 Jewish men, women, and children had found a violent death. Whoever survived was sent, in cattle trains, to labor camps to be annihilated by hunger, disease, and exposure to the elements."

Les stopped for a moment, noticing how deeply his story touched me, my eyes moist. Then, he said, thoughtfully; "General Antonescu put his country on top of an infamous list. Ahead of Nazi Germany, it received first place on the list of unspeakable atrocities and cruelties committed by a country in the course of the genocide. Second to Nazi Germany, Romania, as a country, exterminated the largest number of Jewish civilians during the Second World War.

However, by 1943, Antonescu started to read the clear signs of German defeat. In hope of saving his country and himself from reprisals, he attempted to approach the Allies and switch sides. As a part of these efforts, the anti-Semitic activities were reduced and the lives of many Jews were spared, especially in Bucharest where the exposure to public scrutiny could not be stopped."

"What happened to him?" I asked.

"The end of Antonescu was not good," Les answered.

"When the Russian army regrouped and turned towards the Romanian borders, its king signed an armistice agreement with the Soviets, attempting to spare the capital from destruction. In spite of this, the Russian army entered Bucharest, 'liberating' it from German presence, as well as from its former leaders. The king sought and found refuge in Greece, with his royal Greek relatives; and Antonescu was executed in jail. He hoped to be given the last honor, as was deserved by a General, and to be put in front of a military firing squad; however, his end came unceremoniously by the hands of the local jail guards.

A new leadership was chosen. It was selected and approved by the Soviet Central Committee, and it brought a new era to Romania—Communism."

"O.K., Les, whatever you are telling is very interesting, although depressing, but how do I fit into this picture?" I asked.

He answered; "During this period, the U.S. tried to stay involved, keeping a finger on the pulse and ready to step in whenever possible. The wealth of oil and other mineral resources in Romania had many American venture capitalists salivating over the enormous potential profits buried underground. Official, semi-official, and private delegations scuttled continuously between the two continents, and only Romania realignment with the Axis powers interrupted this stream. It was replaced by intelligence activities, conducted by the newly created American spying cadre, the Overseas Strategic Services, known as O.S.S., under the auspices of its mentor, the British spying apparatus. The Romanian operation started as a small network of agents and informers, their main assignment being to report from behind enemy lines. However, with the collapse of the Nazi supported regime and the transfer of power to Soviet authorities, it became a full and visible presence. Allied with the winning side, the intelligence activities were conducted out in the open, in parallel and in coordination with the agencies of other winning allies."

Les stopped. I used the opportunity to get up, stretch and to tell Les;" Let me get another couple of beers."

I brought them back and encouraged Les to continue, after taking few sips. He did;

"One of the agents recruited locally, who was liked and favored by most of the American operatives, was a young man in his thirties, Jacques Debarbanel.

He was said to be handsome, outgoing, smart, and have a good sense of humor. He always had a joke or an amusing anecdote to use whenever tension rose, or when opportunities called for it. Jacques was fluent in English, French, and German, in addition to his mother language, Romanian. He was well groomed, proud of his looks, and vain enough to tell close friends that his wish was to die and be remembered as a young and handsome man, rather than to get old and wilted.

Ironically, his wish was fulfilled.

Jacques was extremely resourceful and full of initiative. Not sticking to his formal education in accounting, he constantly scouted for ways and connections to improve his living conditions, deteriorated by the scarcities of the war and by his problem."

"What was his problem?" I asked.

There was one big problem with Jacques; he was Jewish."

"But why do you tell me stories about him?" I asked.

"Because it has to do a lot with you. Just be patient and listen, and please try not to interrupt me so much. I promise it will all be clear to you shortly," was his answer. Then, he kept talking, this time without any interruptions;

"Born in the northern city of Iasi, he came as a student to Bucharest, where he established his permanent home. He married a young lady who had arrived, together with her mother and two sisters, from the northern territories taken by Romania from the remains of the Austro-Hungarian Empire.

The young couple watched with horror at the atrocities committed against their religion, family, and friends. Then news started to arrive. Jacques's family in Iasi was decimated. One of his brothers was taken to a labor camp, from which he escaped and disappeared in the vastness of Eastern Europe. The handicapped wife of the same brother remained in town, together with a daughter who took care of her. Both were raped and murdered in their own home in broad daylight. Jacques's wife lost her father and a sister. They were taken to a hard labor camp in Transnistria, where they perished. Numerous friends and distant relatives vanished, never to be heard from again.

Jacques himself was accidentally saved from the massacre in Bucharest. While it took place he was in a local labor camp, performing compulsory public work after being rounded up by the Iron Guard. His wife went to live with friends in the city, waiting for her husband to come back. On the way, she encountered a crowd of rowdy anti-Semitic demonstrators en route to another act of vandalism. She quickly pulled a head scarf from her purse, covered her head in the fashion of a Romanian peasant women—a fashion inherited from the long years of Ottoman occupation—and joined the crowd, raising her fist in unison with them while they shouted, 'kill the Jews!' She could not mutter one word; she knew her accent would give her away. At a street corner she retreated into a courtyard, hid behind a pile of rubble, and waited till it was safe to reach her destination.

When the couple returned back to their home they found it ransacked, and most of their neighbors had been murdered."

Lester took a sip from his beer bottle and continued;

"One of the liaisons Jacques developed was with a young Romanian military pilot, Ionel Popescu, annexed to a German squadron. The pilot, a Romanian patriot but not a supporter of the Nazi cause, found a way to satisfy his frustrations, together with his material needs. Each time he came back from a sortie, he brought with him a large industrial roll of undeveloped film, supplied by the Germans to all mission planes to film and document up to three continuous hours of combat or other aerial activity. In Bucharest, the civilian market was completely dry of filming and photography supplies; such merchandise was in high demand. Looking for a venue to capitalize on his self-awarded prize, Popescu approached Jacques and a business venture was created. Whenever the pilot came back with a roll, he would meet Jacques and give it to him. Jacques then took the large roll into an improvised dark room in his kitchen, separated it into small segments, and transformed it into close to 3000 regular film rolls, which sold in the clandestine market of contraband goods. The proceeds were split, creating a source of income for both men.

This additional source of income had some strings of danger attached- if discovered, both partners could face a military tribunal with predictable sentences of execution, for pilferage of military equipment. One night, Jacques came close to such fate. On the way home, after meeting the pilot and receiving a new airplane film roll, his little capricious car had a flat tire. While Jacques was in the process of changing the tire, he spotted two militia men riding their horses in his direction. He knew he might be carded and then his car searched. The large roll of film, encased in an aluminum cover bearing the symbol of the Luftwaffe, the German air force, and a big swastika, laid on the passenger seat, in full view. He decided quickly what to do. He stood up and started waving furiously at the two militia men, signaling to them to come towards him. They came and dismantled their horses, the band of their brown shirts sleeves displaying their affiliation to the Iron Guard. 'Good evening, guys, I am so happy to see you. I need help' Jacques said. 'How about making some extra money for helping me change this damn tire?'

"How much will you give us for our help?" one of them asked, with a heavy peasant accent.

"Enough to buy you two good meals and a bottle of wine," answered Jacques, taking out all the cash he had in his pockets.

The militia men looked at each other, tied their horses to a tree, waved Jacques aside and proceeded to work for few minutes, completing the changing of the flat tire, while the roll of film was under their nose. When the job was completed they received the cash, thanked Jacques heartily for providing them with a good meal, mounted their horses and disappeared in the darkness.

In no time, Jacques became known in Bucharest's small community of professional photographers. In those times, regular people did not possess cameras. It was a prized and expensive piece of equipment and few could afford such a purchase, even when available in the market. Besides, the cameras in existence took a lot of skill to maneuver the lenses for distance, focus, light, and exposure time for each shot. Then even if these obstacles were overcome, there were no commercial labs to develop the film except in individually improvised dark rooms, which required special skills. A new profession of photographers emerged, which combined all three ingredients together. The only thing these professionals lacked was the raw material, the regular film. Jacques became their provider.

A Romanian, who worked with the Americans and was a distributor of Jacques's goods, introduced Jacques to Oscar, the head of the American network in Bucharest.

Oscar recruited Jacques for an assignment where he was required to get as much information as possible from the Romanian pilot and, if possible, to recruit him as well. Jacques, aware of the pilot's increasing dissatisfaction with the Germans, took the risk and succeeded in recruiting him, but the handling was given to an intelligence officer at the mission.

As a reward, Oscar made Jacques his assistant, needing his language skills. A relationship of friendship and mutual respect developed between them, and it was only a matter of time before Jacques became Oscar's right arm and confidant.

The head of the O.S.S. network in Bucharest conducted his daily activities, as well as a multitude of social ones, out of a stately mansion, retrieved from a wealthy Nazi supporter who was no longer around. This beautiful French style residence became the scene of numerous meetings between Americans and Soviets, both sides rubbing shoulders, congratulating each other, and getting drunk on the vast quantity of fine French champagne found in the well stocked wine cellar. Jacques took part in most of these occasions, serving as a translator.

This is how Oscar and Jacques hit a jackpot.

One of the first civilian organizational steps to be taken by the new leadership was to have a population census and to issue new identity cards for the Romanian citizens. While the process went smoothly in Bucharest, the authorities needed professionals for the rest of the country, mainly for the rural areas.

The vast majority of the population lived in small towns, villages, and hamlets detached from the capital. The prevalent lack of infrastructure in Romania was overwhelming; most establishments did not have paved roads connecting to the rest of the country. Some did not even have electricity, running water, or a means of transportation other than horses, mules, and animal-pulled carts. Their inhabitants heard the news through the grapevine only, as there were no radios. It was the first time an identity card with an identifying picture was being issued to people who had never had their picture taken before.

With Oscar pulling some strings and warm recommendations from the professional photographer community, Jacques Debarbanel was assigned the task of supplying the photographs of the rural people. For this purpose he was paired with a government statistician, provided a vehicle, appropriate empowering documents, and sent on the road.

For more than a year, Jacques traveled through the most remote parts of the country. Whenever he came back to restock and spend few days with his family, he brought a wealth of intelligence to the American mission: numbers, attitudes, political inclinations, infrastructure, and other information, which provided a first-hand source and assessment not available to even the Romanian government officials. His harvest became a primary ingredient in the American action-taking decisions. He also liked to tell numerous stories about his adventures and experiences while on the road."

"What kind of stories?" I asked, this time completely sincere about my curiosity.

"Many stories," was his answer.

"He told a story about one wintry snowy night when driving from one remote village to another, they lost their way in the middle of a forest. He and his companion spent the whole night inside the car freezing, while the car itself was surrounded by a howling pack of wolves attracted by the prospect of some fresh meat. Pairs of glowing red eyes, moving constantly around, were the only thing they could see in the surrounding darkness. In the morning, they were found by searching villagers, and the snow that accumulated around the car throughout the night was stamped with numerous pairs of paws. His young companion's hair had turned completely white overnight.

And the time when their car got stuck on a dirt road that had been washed away by torrential rain, which created an ocean of mud. The spinning wheels buried the car to the axle and a tree root punctured the gas tank, its contents spilling and leaving it dry. A horse rider passing by summoned the neighboring villagers. They showed up shortly after with a pair of oxen and ropes. The car arrived to the main square of the village, the triumphant villagers leading the oxen. Jacques was behind the steering wheel and the gasless car advanced slowly, tied in ropes to the pulling beasts.

Other more humorous stories were about the warm receptions waiting for him. Villagers used to put on a feast to show their hospitality, gratitude, and respect for the honorees from the big city. In these feasts, the local wine poured like water and the evenings, lit mostly by candles and kerosene lamps, ended with the hosts falling asleep drunk in the alleys and the dirt roads of the village.

Or there was the story of the pig. On one of the trips, on a road leading to a god forsaken hamlet, a pig scurried in front of the car, like being chased by the devil. Too late to react, the car hit the pig, which turned on its back in the middle of the road, blocking it while squealing. Suddenly, a peasant came running from one of the houses. He took a quick look at the wounded pig and at the car and its drivers. Without a word, he turned on his heels, hurrying back into the house. A moment later he emerged again, this time holding a large butcher knife in his hand. He kept running towards the car. Jacques and his companion were terrified. However, the peasant stopped in front of the car, approached the pig, bent over and with a quick slash across the throat slaughtered it. He explained to the astonished onlookers that this was his original intent and the accident only precipitated his action. The two travelers were too shocked to continue. They turned around and that particular hamlet never made it into the official annals of Romania.

He told stories about families of gypsies he met on the dirt tracks. They were traveling from one place to another in horse drawn wagons containing all their possessions looking for temporary employment in their constant wandering, offering their skills in music and fortune telling. Many evenings were spent in the company of these musicians, 'lautari,' who displayed amazing virtuosity without reading one note. Jacques was so impressed he used every opportunity to be taught by them to play the fiddle.

Some villagers were afraid to have their picture taken for religious and superstitious reasons. Taking a picture was like taking a part of the soul and only the village chief could convince or force them to comply. The national liquor, 'tuica,' a highly alcoholic version of plum cognac, was another tool of persuasion. Many of the pictures depicted completely stoned faces and rolled eyes, the subjects being too drunk to control their facial expressions. He brought back from one of his trips a picture of a young and robust peasant who was smiling. It was a golden smile. Wanting to gain the favors of a young village girl, he took all his savings and went to the local dentist. There the dentist tried to convince him he had the most beautiful and healthy set of teeth. It did not help. The dentist ended up pulling all his front teeth, upper and lower, and replaced them with gold teeth, a symbol of wealth.

These stories, told and retold in different versions, became a constant source of amusement for the Americans as well as their Russian guests, and Jacques became a favorite at their social gatherings.

What disturbed Jacques the most about these new identity cards was that they bore anti-Semitic seeds. The communist regime, claiming all citizens were equal, the one to crush religion and build a secular society, did not forget the Jews. Their identity cards included one more word; 'mosaic,' indicating they belonged to the faith of Moses.

He mentioned this fact to Oscar, in one of his briefings. Oscar looked at him and said, using the Americanized version of his name; "Jack, if we succeed in our mission, I'll make sure you and your family get American passports and you could come to America, where nobody cares what you are."

Jacques answered with sad sarcasm; "Thanks, Oscar. It sounds great and I know you mean what you say. However, this is what I think; If we succeed, your people will call me 'the New American,' the Romanians will call me 'the Great Citizen' and the world will see me as a great patriot. But if you fail, the Americans will call me 'a Romanian' and the Romanians will call me 'just another Jew', while the world turns its back to my tragic prognosis."

The fraternity between Russians and Americans in Bucharest was short lived. It dissipated when reality hit and Romania took the clear path leading to the Soviet Union, preparing to become one of its satellites. The American intelligence mission, without a clear directive from the top administration, started covert activities targeted at undermining the Soviet influence and changing the balance of political parties.

It was the first time that an American entity, designated to collect and transfer intelligence and still in its infancy, stepped into the territory of covert operations. They used the British tradition of meddling in the internal matters of other countries, but with complete lack of experience. Secretly, it encouraged a major political Romanian party to oppose the Russian influence. The plan was to create a political coalition in which the O.S.S. supported party was a major player. Then Romania could be steered away from the Reds and redirect its orientation westward, or at least, stay neutral, like the newly created country of Yugoslavia, a confederation of few smaller countries with diverse groups of minorities.

In this spirit, the American top intelligence officials streamed a constant flow of funds, weapons, and propaganda material to a newly created underground for a period of a few months. Being planned by such debutants, it did not take too long before the plot was discovered by the Soviet authorities. The leaders of the straying party and other members of the underground were arrested and most of them executed. The ones left alive were sent to hard labor camps to use shovels and buckets to build a canal in the Danube Delta, a place from which nobody came back. Others were crowded into troop carrier trains and shipped to the vast Soviet wilderness.

The American mission folded.

Oscar and the American members of the mission evacuated as fast as they could, taking with them a few Romanians they could save, realizing that those they left behind would perish.

One of the casualties was Ionel Popescu, the Romanian pilot.

Another victim of this fiasco was Jacques Debarbanel.

He was arrested in the final hours before the American evacuation, while trying to get into the mission's mansion. His last words to the helpless staff, watching behind the ornamented wrought iron fence, as he was dragged into a Soviet military truck, were; 'save my family."

Lester stopped and then he said; "This was the last time anybody saw Jacques, your father."

He was looking at me, waiting for his words to sink in.

I sat in complete silence.

After a while, as I was just about to open my mouth, Les silenced me and said; "Just let me finish...

Oscar, the head of the O.S.S. mission heard the ply. He devoted some of his last hours on Romanian soil trying to do something. Only one member of his family could be saved. The infant boy, given to a couple of cooperators claiming he was their baby, was transported to the border and from there smuggled to Vienna, Austria.

This is how you arrived to the Soviet-free world."

I was trying to open my mouth, but Les stopped me and said; "Just one more minute...

Oscar watched with terrible feelings of guilt at the cleansing in Romania. From the safety of his new offices in Vienna, he tried to help his former associates, but they were beyond reach. For the ones who escaped, he committed to help and rebuild their ruined lives on safer shores. They were given special passing documents and most of them reached the States.

Oscar took a special interest in the infant. In the following years he allocated special funds to ensure Jacques Debarbanel's son would grow up in a safe home, with a trust reserved for his future education.

By then Oscar had become a senior officer in the new outfit, the C.I.A. In this capacity, he took an active role in the creation of the Marshall Plan.

The Plan was the result of the American determination to protect additional European countries from following the Red path. The administration made enormous amounts of money available that were put at the disposal of these countries for reconstruction purposes. The only condition was each country would match these funds with their own resources, while the management was left to local officials. Seizing the opportunity, the top officers of the C.I.A. convinced the leadership of these countries to create special secret funds and reserves to be transferred to the covert operators of the Agency. Enormous discretionary funds resulted. Most of the secret funds were used to build caches of weapons to be left with the local underground, formed and nourished to fight Communism. Some of the funds were used to rebuild and secure the future of the European collaborators who found refuge in the West, including you. Oscar received periodical reports about your progress. When the time arrived, he was instrumental in having you employed by the pharmaceutical company, the C.I.A. front, it too a fruit of these funds."

Lester finished.

I sat completely quiet for a while, overwhelmed with emotions, a knot in my throat stopping the tears starting to form in my moist eyes.

I got up on my feet and told Lester; "Les, I am speechless. I need to digest all this. I need some time. My goodness, you just opened a window to a new world.

Do you know how to reach me?"

He smiled, got up, put a hand on my shoulder, and said; "I understand and I do expect you to take some time to think it over. I know how to get hold of you. With your permission, I'll contact you in a couple of weeks."

He turned around getting ready to leave, and then, remembering something, he sat down again, signaling me to do the same. He stuck his hand into the inside pocket of his jacket and while his fingers were searching, he said; "I almost forgot. I have a little present for you."

He pulled out a photo and put it on the table.

It was a picture of Les and me in Managua, showing two younger, tanned, smiling fellows. I looked at it, memories coming back, while Les was observing me.

Then his hand moved quickly back into the same pocket and retrieved another older sepia colored picture. It showed a young man with a familiar face. Les put the two pictures next to each other, and then I realized I was looking at a slightly different version of myself. The resemblance was unmistakable.

For the first time, I was looking at my father.

Les, observing the recognition in my eyes, pushed them to me and said; "Please, keep them both. I found this photo in your father's file, and I knew that one day it would belong to you."

He stood up again, and I did the same.

We shook hands and I watched as Lester started walking, with his slight limp, toward the exit, then disappeared into the airport crowds.

As I turned to look back, I saw he left behind the package he came with. I opened the string and looked at its contents. In it I found the machete that almost took my life in Nicaragua. A note was attached to it; 'I kept it for many years. Now it is yours.'

It still hangs as an ornament on a wall in my little home study, a constant reminder of how frail and unpredictable life is and how strong and reliable friendship can be.

When he called two weeks later asking for a meeting, I turned down his offer over the phone.

I could not tell him why and I did not want to lie.

I could not tell him that I knew this story already, indeed in a much shorter, concise, and dry version, without too many personal details. It was told to me by a high ranking C.I.A. officer on assignment to recruit me. It was accompanied by some words from the grave, a letter written many years before by Oscar meant to be given to me at the right time. The letter that told me how much my father's friendship had meant to him and the sorrow he felt for not being able to save his life.

The time had come for the Company to get back what it paid for.

This was the man who convinced me to join the Company as a freelancer, part of an internal unit in charge of spying on its own personnel to detect moles and agents selling secrets. A unit known to a handful of top ranking officials only.

It was not a full-time job, at least not at the beginning, and it did not interfere with my regular business trips. On the contrary, they were my natural cover for information gathering during my overseas trips.

It became a full-time job after 2003.

My boss, the Head of the Special Internal and Inter-Agencies Affairs, was assigned to collect ALL information related to the TRUE events surrounding 9/11. I was part of his small team, all of us having kept low profiles and being basically unknown to the members of the intelligence community.

As I told Les, I did have a middle age change of careers. Just different from what I led him to think.

The next time I saw Lester was fifteen years later, in the West Side Loony House.

SECOND VISIT

I retuned to the mental institution two days later. I needed the time to set up a few things and to establish some objectives with my immediate superior, while I waited for good weather. The second meeting had to take place outside. I had to stick to my assignment; to make Lester Ross talk in a place he did not feel like he was being watched.

Before going to the attendants' station I made a stop in the public restrooms. I was overcome with disgust at the sight of the filth and the sickening smells. Entering one of the stalls, I opened my briefcase and put the medical white coat on top of my business suit. I took out the stethoscope, part of my disguise, and I wrapped it around my neck, its listening end tucked in the left upper pocket of the coat. Before leaving, I took a quick glance at myself in the stained and smeared mirror. I liked the reflection- tall, slim although not muscular, grey receding hair appropriate for a middle age guy, rimless eyeglasses, it all added to the look of a professional. Yes, I definitely looked like a doctor.

The attendant who took me to Lester's room was the same as two days ago, and he kept busy reporting Les's behavior, which according to him was low on the scale of lunacy.

I was nice to him this time. I extended my arm and said with a friendly voice; "You can call me Robert. What is your name?"

He shook my hand and said; "My name is Joshua. Please call me Josh, and I am pleased to meet you."

He was not surprised when, after hearing him, I told him my plans for the day; to spend a considerable amount of time with the patient outside in the hospital garden, unaccompanied and without restraints. "More than anything else, I need complete privacy and no disturbances. You don't come to us, we come to you, when I am done," I told him.

The attendant nodded, agreeing to my requirements but he said; "You are playing with fire. These psychos are unpredictable and can turn on you in one instant."

"Believe me I know what I am doing, and besides, I am the clinical expert, not you," I answered, putting an end to his attempts to patronize me.

I entered Les's room. He was seated, unrestrained, smiling at us both, evidently hearing my last words. The attendant was waiting, next to me, as I had previously instructed.

"Les, today we are going to spend some time outside. The weather is beautiful, this place has a nice backyard, and I brought some subs with me, so we can have a meal in the fresh air. This gentleman," I said, "will take us outside and then leave us alone. Please promise him you'll behave."

Les raised his right arm and with a comical boy-scout gesture, said; "I promise to behave."

The attendant took us outside, to a large garden in the back of the building. At one time it was manicured, surrounded by an impressive wrought iron decorative fence. Now it was neglected, its overgrown grass covering most of the trails. The fence was replaced by a brick wall, separating the world from the nightmares and misery on its premises. I directed us to an isolated spot close to the wall where a picnic table and two benches were installed the previous day, per my instructions.

I dismissed the attendant, telling him to give us two hours of complete privacy, and both of us sat, facing each other, with the table separating between us.

"All right, Les," I said when we were left alone. "Let's talk about you now. Tell me what the hell you are doing here and please cut all nonsense."

He looked at me for a long time and, making up his mind, he said; "This is my refuge, Robert. It is the one place where I feel safe. It took me a long time to decide what would be the best place to hide and, believe me, there is no such place. So while I think about a better alternative, this is my new address."

"Who are you hiding from, and why?" I asked, pretending, quite convincingly, to have a complete lack of knowledge.

"Robert, are you sure you want to get into this mess? You know my occupation and the hazards associated to it. Don't you realize that sometimes knowing too much could be dangerous for your health— your life actually?"

"Les, I am a clinical psychiatrist, licensed by the State Board to listen, with complete confidentiality, to all my patients. Unless a crime is about to be committed and could be prevented, nobody can ask me any questions about my patients; and I have the duty to protect their secrets. So you can rest assured that nobody can induce, intimidate, threaten, or tempt me to say one word about our conversations. It is my professional duty to protect your privacy. Moreover, I don't even intend to take any notes, so what I hear here, stays here."

Lies, lies.

Lester kept quiet for few seconds, digesting my arguments. Then, looking straight into my eyes, said; "O.K…I think I am ready, if you have the time and patience to listen."

"Try me, Les," I said.

My strategy worked. I was, hopefully, just about to hear what knowledge caused him to seek shelter in such an unlikely place and what caused him to fear for his life.

He took a long breath and started talking;

"Robert, I am about to spill my guts and expose you to a lot of information. I need, once again, to make sure you have the time and inclination to listen, without prejudice. Otherwise, you might reach the conclusion I belong here and I am hallucinating or suffering from deep mental disorders like paranoia, schizophrenia, or whatever name you psychiatrists can think of."

"Les, I have all the time in the world, and I am ready to listen to you for days. I promise also not to make any presumption before you finish," I answered.

Lester kept quiet for a while and then, looking with a sudden sharp look at me, asked;

"By the way, Robert, I have been here for almost two weeks. How come you just found out about my presence here? Besides, I thought that by now I met all the medical staff, till you showed up."

"Les, are you becoming really paranoid? What kind of question is this?" I answered. "I am a resident doctor in the outpatient department, and I don't think you were treated there, because I would have known, and you would have seen me. Hey, if you don't feel comfortable talking to me, lets just finish the sandwiches and go back inside. By the way" I said, pulling pay stub from my wallet, which had a plastic window exposing my business card with the name and the 'DR., Clinical Psychiatry' attached. "I just received my last pay and let me tell you, it is not fun being a resident doctor. I think I could make more money in a burger joint."

I had done my homework. I knew the institution has an outpatient department with completely different staff, and the inpatients don't have access to any information regarding that department.

My reaction, a rehearsed one for the eventuality that such doubt might rise, put him at ease. He made a motion, ignoring the fake stub, to put my wallet back.

He nodded with his head accepting my explanation and reaction, then remembering his professional routine, got up and started searching behind the bushes separating the wall from our sitting spot. It took a while. Satisfied that nobody and no listening devices are hidden, he returned to the table, sat and started talking. While he was going through this routine I was thinking that anybody watching him looking around, bending down, shaking the bushes and touching the leaves, received an additional reinforcement to his insanity. But, I knew better- he was suspicious and precautious.

"So what would you like to talk about?" I revived the conversation.

"The subject is the 9/11 events and the truth, as I know it," he started.

This was, indeed, what I hoped to hear; the purpose of my assignment.

My strategy was to be skeptical, challenge statements made, and ask for evidence, especially names and documents if they were in existence, by asking the right questions, at the right time.

"Is this truth different from the one I know?" I asked him.

"Yes. Very much so. What you know is not the truth," he answered.

"Les, this is a bad start already," I said. "Let me tell you first what I think about the subject, so you know where I stand. While I don't have any doubts about your sanity, I have my reservations and you'll need to use all your arguments and input to convince me otherwise. I have heard numerous comments of disbelief about the official version and some of the 'conspiracy' theories before. Truthfully, being involved in my own world and tending to rely on public media, I have not given much thought to the matter.

Moreover, people raising doubts have been treated with discern, trying to slaughter the holiest cows of the nation. A person can become extremely unpopular when expressing any doubts about the official stories. Friends would ridicule. Business associates or employers would cut such conversations short and never give another chance to renew them. Who in his or her right mind can even think something different, like a cover-up, or even worse, an American conspiracy, could be behind this immense national tragedy? Even mentioning the slightest doubt can be considered a blasphemy, an insult to the innocent civilian victims and their families. Besides, it is just so much easier to go with the flow rather than straining my gray matter and trying to dig, unnecessarily, into the unreachable unknown."

I just planted the carefully prepared bait, challenging Les from the very beginning, putting him on defense, pressing him for convincing arguments and facts. He took it.

Les said gravely; "For your information, at this very moment, a large percentage of the Americans is convinced the truth is different from what they know. There are just too many people who put the little shards of unmatching information together and reached the same conclusion; they are lied to and misled. Many books, articles, and commentaries were written and movies were made, depicting the improbability of the official version. There are pending law suits in Federal courts, brought by families of some of the victims requesting the real truth, not accepting the official version given. Every major city in the States has been the scene of demonstrations and conventions requesting explanations beyond the official one. They know something is wrong; they just don't know what, why, and who. When there are so many something must be behind it. Don't you agree?"

I nodded and he took my nod as a sign to continue; "I am perfectly aware that even talking about these events, without expressing complete consensus with the official version, constitutes a moral assault on thousands of people who were directly affected.

From the other hand, I know they deserve to know the truth, even when it is a bitter one. Truth is not necessarily a pleasant thing."

"Les," I said, "You know my admiration for you and my eternal gratitude for saving my life. I'll listen with an open mind and infinite patience to whatever you want me to hear. But I have to tell you upfront, it will be an impossible task to convince me that my government, my leaders, misled me and my fellow people and fed us false information, or even worse, had anything to do with this. Actually, now as I am talking and thinking about it at the same time, I do believe it is even unpatriotic to listen, never mind talking, about such an improbable, unlikely, and yes, insane subject. I have to tell myself I am a clinical psychiatrist to be able to listen to this. Besides, I thought you intend to talk about your mental issues, maybe intimate matters you don't feel comfortable discussing with strangers. You really surprise me saying you want to discuss politics and giving me the understanding they are the reason for your institutionalization here. If the subject is the one you mentioned, why did you pick me as your confidant?"

Les looked at me and weighing his words, said; "I have three grown up children. They are mature persons by now, with their own families. When you reach such a stage in life, Robert, people closest to you react in ways different than expected. In my children's eyes, I am a fossil, part of an aging generation. My knowledge and experience is ridiculed and then ignored. The only time they might listen to anything I have to say is when they are in some kind of trouble or in need of some assistance nobody else other than me could give. My wife of many years is in her own world. She is not interested in any version of the truth that deviates from the main stream. She accepts whatever she hears and I feel it is a waste of time, hers and mine, to have her listen. When I attempted to test her reactions in the past, she told me flat out my occupation transformed me into a paranoid person and she is not ready even to hear me talk. So, I gave up on my family. As per present or former associates, I could endanger them. They took their oath and should not be put in a position to breach it."

After a while, looking to a distant point above my head, he continued;

"I am going to give you a long, but necessary, dissertation about the main players before we get into the events themselves. You have to be patient, and then the picture will become clear. I'll try to explain why and how our government has become an enormous accumulation of conflicting interests, opposing positions, and different perceptions of reality, all clashing with each other. Politicians, the military, bureaucrats, and the media have been engaged in a race for dominance and influence, marked by intrigue, betrayals, and constant re-alliances. The constantly growing high stakes they have been playing are the only motivation and for their action, in complete disregard to the public interest and well being"

My face probably showed confusion, so Les said; "I guess you realized by now my level of respect for our politicians is as low as it could be, so let's start with a joke: Two guys are arguing in a bar. A bystander sipping his cocktail hears one of the arguing men exclaiming, 'all politicians are crooks!' The bystander turns and says, 'excuse me, sir, I disagree with you and I take this as a personal insult.' 'Why?' asks the man. 'Are you a politician?' 'God forbid,' answers the bystander. 'I am a crook.'

Then, he changed his sitting position and began speaking in a lecturing tone; "The first player I am putting on the stage is the Central Intelligence Agency. The C.I.A. is only one of the entities that comprise the American 'intelligence community.' There are at least sixteen intelligence agencies which are part of this 'community.' N.S.A. is still the largest of all, in spite of the fact that there is little known about it. This is such a secretive organization that outsiders claim the initials, N.S.A., stand for 'Never Such Agency,' while the insiders claim they stand for 'Never Say Anything.' Even the military has its own intelligence. We have the N.G.I.A., which stands for National Geospatial Intelligence Agency, in charge of topographical and photographical surveillance and analysis; and the D.I.A., Defense Intelligence Agency, conducting military human intelligence activities. Then there is the National Reconnaissance Office, a late comer into the community established after the space invasion, providing satellite images on the ground. We have intelligence units which are part of the F.B.I., the State Department, The Bureau of Arms, Tobacco, and Firearms, known as A.T.F., the Drug Enforcement Agency, known as D.E.A., the Department of Homeland Security, the Treasury Department, the Energy Department, and so on.

The C.I.A., the Central Intelligence Agency or The Company, as it is better known, was created immediately following the Second World War, as a successor to another organization, O.S.S. The initials stood for Overseas Strategic Services, the first American attempt to have an entity dedicated to collecting overseas intelligence."

"Why did you start with all this history?" I interrupted him.

"Because I believe this is the only way for you to understand the whole picture," he answered.

I did not try to contradict him, or tell him I already knew all these facts and even more, so I nodded in agreement encouraging him to continue, which he did.

"The traditional philosophy of isolationism, which characterized the American policy toward the rest of the world till the First World War, had not justified any formalization of intelligence collection, or in other words, spying on other countries. The basic fact that the U.S. was a continent away from any other countries, except for Canada and Mexico, created the serenity and peace of mind that the country could not be, from a practical point of view, attacked or surprised by an invasion. Even after the end of this war and the emergence of the Soviet empire, intelligence activities were conducted as a by-product of international diplomacy by the State Department, through its embassies and consulates wherever they existed. These activities could be characterized as being naïve, rudimentary, and lacking any sophistication or depth. This, in complete contrast to the Europeans who, due to centuries old rivalries between the various countries and monarchies, had developed sophisticated spying and intelligence traditions and tools. Only the start of the Second World War and the increasing dependency of American policymakers on intelligence, obtained mainly from the spying agencies of Great Britain, resulted in the creation of O.S.S., and it was the first time ever a civil entity was given such responsibilities."

"So, we never spied on other people," I said. "These are good news, to know we mind our own business. But, how did we gather knowledge about our enemies?" I asked.

Les answered; "In times of war, it was the duty of the military to collect intelligence, and the Pentagon fed and nourished few intelligence entities. Belonging to different military branches, these intelligence gathering divisions did not cooperate and did not share the fruits of their labor, sometimes even spying on each other.

From its very beginning, O.S.S. was controversial. As far as its mentors—the British intelligence—regarded it, the new organization was a bunch of debutants. On the U.S. side, it created animosity and friction with the American military, which saw in the new outfit an attempt to limit and interfere, an attempt most unwelcome. The fact that the teachers, instructors, and mentors of the O.S.S. agents were British was of tremendous relevance later when these operatives were transferred into the newly created C.I.A.; and one by one became top executives, including some of its Directors, such as Dulles, Helms, and Casey.

The British, with their long tradition of mingling with and ruling foreign countries and transforming them into satellite territories—colonial components of a vast empire—showed their new disciples how to do so as well. The C.I.A. incorporated the concept of ruling and dividing countries in its agenda, and some of its biggest successes were toppling foreign sovereign governments, such as in Iran, Guatemala, and Chile.

Meanwhile, the war was over, but the military and security apparatus and bureaucracy increased, rather than decreasing or disappearing. The end of the war brought a new armed force, the Air Force, a new organization, the C.I.A., and an additional layer of bureaucrats incorporated into the newly created Department of Defense, a buffer between the military and its Commander in Chief, the President of the U.S..

Putting a civil servant on top of the military brass, in between the multi-stared generals and the President, was not received gracefully and has constituted a sore in the Pentagon's eyes, which grew bigger and bigger as the years went by. This fact would come to haunt every administration and have a magnitude of repercussions later on. The original charter of the C.I.A. was to provide intelligence to the President of the U.S. It was not created to police or to fight, these tasks were left to the F.B.I. and the military. However, these boundaries were crossed almost immediately when the trespassers got into subversive activities."

Les took a break, looking at me, trying to see how much I had absorbed. Noticing my sign of approval, he continued; "The end of the war brought Communist regimes to a large number of European countries, and Communist parties flourished freely and legally in many more. The increasing influence of the Soviet Union culminated with the erection of the Berlin Wall, which divided Berlin, Germany, Europe, and actually the entire world into two competing poles of power and political identification and alignment. It created the Cold War. This war validated the need for the C.I.A. services and its popularity, but not without objections.

From its start, by the virtue of its charter and its modus operandi, the C.I.A. stood for whatever was strange and opposite to the spirit of the Pentagon and the F.B.I. Its semi-legal, illegal, and sometimes criminal ways of operations, natural behavior for a spying and subversive operations machine, were not the spirit of the law abiding and enforcing F.B.I. Its lack of clear organizational hierarchy and the loose ways of adopting decisions and implementing them were strange and contradictory to the Pentagon, which was used to the layered military concept and formal procedures.

Soon enough, the red Communist monster started to emerge as the main enemy to the United States and its lifestyle philosophy, capitalism. A new battle cry was heard; Communism is the main threat to the western culture and civilization. Battling the spread of Communism became the main, if not the only, focus of the new agency.

To enhance the importance of its services, the C.I.A. inflated the perception of the mighty Soviet threat, an enhancement which became bolder and more misleading during the last days of the Soviet empire. The imminent threat of Soviet aggressiveness was artificially reported and its military capabilities were exaggerated from the very beginning. I could tell you about intelligence photos showing Soviet tanks divisions deployed close to their borders. A closer look at them would have shown rusted, inoperative, dated equipment, unfit for any military action, and definitely not a threat for us. Later on, when I reviewed some highly classified documents, which, by the way, were later declassified and exposed to public scrutiny, it became clear that a large portion of the intelligence supplied to the decision makers back home was misleading, false, and even fake.

They fed and encouraged fear among the American Administrations and the public. It was the fear the monster created and used by

Americans would turn, like a Frankenstein, against its maker— the Atomic Bomb.

The nuclear weapon became the Golem of Prague."

Another pause.

Les gave another look at me, questioning if he should continue. He did; "It is true that the sphere of activity and influence of the C.I.A. encompassed the entire globe, but in all cases the subject was the spread of the Communist influence and the Soviet threat. When the C.I.A. was active in Southeast Asia, Burma, Laos, Cambodia, Indochina, which became Vietnam, Korea, and Japan, it acted against the spread of Communism. It was the same in the Middle East, including Egypt, Turkey, Lebanon, Syria, and Iran. I should not forget to mention our backyard, the Americas. Cuba, Guatemala, Nicaragua, and Chile bring some unpleasant memories about the heydays of the Company.

These were good days for the C.I.A., a time when it abandoned its original charter to obtain and provide intelligence expanded into clandestine and subversive operations, many questioned and very few properly authorized by administration.

The fight against the Red Evil was the label under which the organization grew, developed, and flourished. Every president, starting with Truman, commissioned clandestine subversive overseas operations, way beyond the original charter and scope of the C.I.A. These activities peaked during the Kennedy administration when dozens were initiated, with the Attorney General, Robert F. Kennedy, being the liaison. The later presidents were not shy either in using the services of the C.I.A."

Les got up, made a few paces, stretched, and came back to sit. "I know this is a lot of heavy stuff, Robert, but it is essential so you could get the entire picture. There is a lot more to come. Can I continue?"

I nodded positively, and he resumed; "The Soviet threat created an American ménage- a-trois; the C.I.A. overseas and the F.B.I. in the States were kept busy by Senator McCarthy, both organizations feeding the military with enemies and military targets for action including: Korea, Vietnam, Laos, Cambodia, Guatemala, Nicaragua, and, of course, don't forget Cuba. Then something bad for these organizations happened. The Wall was brought down. Although it happened after President Reagan said his famous phrase, 'Mr. Gorbatchev bring this Wall down,' it actually fell by itself. It fell not because of defeat from outside enemies, but from inside, the result of the many cracks in the Soviet Empire.

The Cold War was over.

The Soviet Empire crumpled and collapsed, bringing down the communist regime in all the satellite countries known as the East Block. Within a very short period the Red Threat disappeared completely. Many see the lack of foresight of the internal turmoil and the weakness inside the Soviet Empire as a major failure of the C.I.A. Rather, it was a deliberate attempt to hang on, as long as possible, to what had became its main reason for existence.

For the C.I.A. it meant that unless another business opportunity was presented rather quickly, it might become an obsolete organization and lose the connections it had made, if not disappear at all."

Les stopped, looking to see if I was paying full attention to him. Satisfied with my alertness, he asked; "Do you see where this is leading?'

I shrugged, not wanting to interfere with his train of thought.

"The C.I.A. had to redefine itself," he continued. "By then, it became an enormous organization with a multitude of divisions, departments and small interest groups, all secretive by the nature of their activity, completely compartmentalized, to the point that I doubt if anyone could draw an organizational chart to include all the components. In other words, nobody had the whole picture, nor cared about it.

In order to exist and prosper in the new world, this mammoth had to find a new target, a new enemy, to justify its existence and possible expansion.

Internal teams and panels within the agency were created to find these alternate reasons for existence.

Some of these replacement objectives concentrated on chemical, biological, and even nuclear threats to be combated by the C.I.A. Interestingly, international terrorism, Radical Islamic in particular, was a possibility of lower priority, in the first years after the collapse of the Soviet Union.

To make the situation worse, the C.I.A. did not officially have a big boss, a secretary, or an official to solely represent it. Its top official was the D.C.I., who to few years ago was in charge of most intelligence entities and agencies. In addition, the D.C.I. chair had become a musical one as directors came and went, the turnover being high. It did not allow enough time for a director to put up a plan for survival and prosperity. It was up to the organization itself to try to reorganize and regain validity. It had to be done fast, before the realization that it was no longer needed. As one of the powerful persons within the Administration commented, the impression was already created and it would not make any difference if the C.I.A. existed, since so many other intelligence agencies were doing the same.

Many studies conducted by Presidents and the Congress pointed, time and time again, at the duplicity, rival relationships, and even conflicts of interests as well as at the need of major reorganization. It meant merging, reforming, redefining, or even disassembling some of these agencies, the C.I.A. included.

Within its labyrinths, a think tank was created to build a master plan and blueprint for a new C.I.A.

However, what started as an official above- ground coordinated effort evolved into a small group of determined career bureaucrats who took a secret oath to preserve the organization; while all the top officers were spending a few weekly hours treading water in appointed steering committees and joint commissions, without making any progress.

I was nominated the coordinator of this team.

In this capacity, I had the opportunity and the responsibility to review dozens of plans, each one analyzed and rated accordingly. There is no point to bore you with details about the intrigues, little internal conspiracies, and the leaks coming from this group. Many influences tried to dominate the outcome and it was my main responsibility to keep the target clear ahead of us. Finally, the group came up with a good plan, after analyzing a bunch, some of them completely insane.

It was a concise plan of action to be translated into covert, subversive, and disinformation activities. It included a few basic principles and guidelines: have an enemy easy to hate, big and threatening enough as to justify the existence and dedication of an organization such as the C.I.A. at its present size or even bigger; can be identified territorially as to keep the military in business, have a domestic U.S. aspect, a fifth column, to keep the F.B.I. busy; be feasible and implemental, considering the resources available; and have an icon who is easy to identify and hate. Remember, the public and the media need an icon, good or bad. We have had plenty of bad icons in the past; Stalin, Hitler, Ho-Chi-Ming, Mao-Tze-Tung, Castro, Saddam Hussein and you could add a few more names to this list.

The end result was good, very good indeed; one single package incorporating all of above. It was the Radical Islam concept that included the bad guys, Al-Qaeda, international and domestic terrorism, Afghanistan as enemy territory, domestic cells in the U.S. and other countries aligned with America, and, of course, an evil icon— Osama Bin Laden."

I thought he finished, as he took a break. I was just about to open my mouth, but noticing, he raised his arm and stopped me.

"I am not done yet. Let me say a few words about the F.B.I., which, by the way, is an enormous organization, substantially bigger size-wise than the C.I.A."

My face did not disclose any objection, letting him to keep building his case.

I was determined to listen, for as long as it took, till he divulged the more specific information, the purpose of my assignment.

Les continued; "The F.B.I. had the same problem as the C.I.A.; once the target of the Communist threat to the heartland was eliminated, it needed to redefine and reinvent itself. The organization, in spite of being sandwiched between state police systems domestically and the C.I.A. overseas, was kept quite busy throughout its one hundred year history. I'll mention the Red Alert era of McCarthy shortly, but let me remind you of a big one before that, the Prohibition era. During those years, in the 1920s, enforcing Prohibition laws under the Federal jurisdiction were golden days of growth and power for the F.B.I. But here we are, in a time when it is legal to drink yourself to death, even in public, provided you are of age; many do so. Here we are when Communism sounds like an old fashioned trend from the past, more remembered by the Baby Boomers, the geriatric club members.

These could have been bad days for the F.B.I., but they were not. It kept itself busy with two new public enemies. The first one has been illegal drug trafficking. This is definitely not my field of expertise, assuming I even have one. However, it is my strong opinion the F.B.I. has conducted a very tough war against a tough enemy, although it has been on the losing side, so far. However, I have my theory for this lack of success, and I might even share it with you one of these days.

It is definitely not the appropriate tine now. The second public enemy which replaced the Communist spies' threat for America was the domestic ultra-right militia, the neo-fascist white supremacist groups, and other radical fringe movements. Some of the methods the F.B.I. used to fight this enemy look like they were taken from an old Hoover manual of covert operations and disinformation.

However, it did an overkill on this enemy, such as Ruby Ridge incident in 1992, when F.B.I. agents shot and killed a family, including a child, and in Waco, Texas, where close to one hundred people, united around their prophet, died; some of them burnt after a siege, followed by an assault waged by the F.B.I. I will not even mention some other incidents rumored to be authored by F.B.I. There are plenty of stories and interpretations of events depicting F.B.I. as the behind the scene manipulator. Some even go to the extreme to accuse F.B.I. as taking part or hiding the truth behind Oklahoma City bombing in 1995. I don't even want to go into the validity of such claims, so well defined as 'conspiracy theories,' because I am an outsider to that organization and I want to concentrate on our subject only.

In any case, lately we don't hear much, if at all, about these movements in the U.S. They still exist and are active; the latest attack, by a white supremacist, at the Memorial Holocaust Museum in D.C., shows what they are capable of doing. White supremacy, neo-Nazis, ultra-right, and racial hate crimes were replaced by the newest public enemy, the infiltrated Radical Muslim terrorists, Al-Qaeda cells, financial backers and supporters, and whatever comes with it."

He took a break, catching his breath. His eyes, usually clear as the blue sky, seemed to concentrate internally on a windmill of thoughts. I took the opportunity to stand up and stretch. When I looked at him again, he was alert and back to his lecturing sitting allure.

But I surprised him and, with a shadow of a smile on my face, I said; "Les, without interrupting the way you build your case, I want to add my little contribution."

It was just the right time to reinforce his determination to go through everything he knew, and he gave me the opening, so I kept going. "What you just described fits exactly into a chapter from my graduate courses in public administration. Is the term 'Parkinson Law' familiar to you?"

"The only Parkinson I am familiar with is the disease my late grandma had," Les said.

"Les, the Parkinson I am talking about was a British guy, and he was one of the first pioneers in the discipline of modern public administration. Will you indulge me?"

Not encountering any resistance or sign of impatience, I started telling him whatever I remembered from my business school days; " Mr. Parkinson lived and worked as a researcher and writer in Great Britain, and he created one of the first case studies in the new field of Public Administration. He spent a few years analyzing the internal structure of the British Ministry of Colonies. Yes, there was such a Ministry.

Parkinson came to a very interesting conclusion; while the colonies were spinning off the British Empire and the Commonwealth was getting smaller, the Ministry, instead of decreasing accordingly, was actually increasing, disproportionately. The number of colonies to be taken care of was smaller and yet new employees were hired and more resources were needed. Parkinson followed the flow of paper—memos, protocols, directives, and the entire bureaucratic machine—and discovered that sometimes these memos ended on empty desks, vacated by the disappearance of the colony itself, with nobody to read them, no actions to be taken, and no problems to solve.

He studied previous cases, as well, in the British Admiralty. In that establishment, the number of the ships in the British Navy decreased by two thirds, and the number of sailors by almost half. At the same time, the number of dockyard workers servicing this fleet skyrocketed and the number of the clerks and beaurocrats more than doubled.

What I am trying to say reinforces your arguments. According to Parkinson, organizations tend to perpetuate and find reasons to exist and prosper, even when there is no more justification. The will to survive becomes the primary target of the public organization, and the original charter becomes irrelevant or is replaced by a more promising other. Officials create work for each other and keep themselves busy, adding as many subalterns they can, each addition making the superior more important within the hierarchy. Even Gorbatchev, the Soviet leader, made once a remark in this spirit. In a discussion with a leader of the Italian Communist Party who complained about the swelling beaurocracy in Italy, he stated,' Parkinson Law works everywhere.'

What you have been saying about the C.I.A. and F.B.I. fits very much into this theory and reinforces it.

How about it?" I ended, with a rhetoric question.

Les listened to me carefully, nodding in approval, and when I finished my little lecture, he seemed quite satisfied.

"Robert," he said. "You don't even realize how much light your little lecture throws on the entire system. This 'law' has so much validity, when looking at these American institutions. It is so true that they stop thinking in terms of national interest and chartered purposes and dedicate their time and resources to self justification and self gratification."

After a while, he collected his thoughts and continued. "If this Parkinson was still alive he could have seen his British Ministry of Colonies was a children's game, when compared with the C.I.A., the F.B.I., and the Pentagon. Which brings me to the next player, the Pentagon."

I had a questioning look in my eyes, so he interrupted his lecturing mode and said;

"Robert, you were a businessman and now you are a doctor. You need all this background in order to see the whole picture."

Then he continued; "A very famous European general said, 'peace is the time between wars.'

This phrase illustrates vividly the military way of thinking and acting. It was created to fight; attack or defend, but fight. In times of peace, the military trains. However, you cannot train for ever; real soldiers are real fighters, and fighters want to fight. The military needs action, and the action is war.

We, Americans have fought a lot. We fought a few wars only to defend our borders; the last wars we fought for our sovereignty were more than a century ago, and even then, they were kind of David and Goliath— one against Mexico and one against the Spanish, when they still ruled Cuba.

The Americans are lucky, not having bad and mean neighbors wishing to attack us. On the contrary, our neighbors love America so much; most of them want to come and live with us here and be like us. They are willing to crawl, walk, run, jump fences, and even swim or row their way in.

So, what to do with this big military machine we kept building until it became a giant? We just have to fight other wars far away from home and from our own borders. Just try to remember how many wars and military actions we conducted in recent memory. We fought two world wars, the First in Europe and the Second in Europe and the Far East at the same time. We fought against the Philippines, Laos, Cambodia, Korea, Vietnam, ex-Yugoslavia, two wars in Iraq, and others in Nicaragua, Guatemala, Dominican Republic, Panama, Granada, Afghanistan. Frankly, I probably forgot one or two others."

"According to you, we love to fight," I interjected.

"It is not for love, but as the reason to exist," he replied, and then, continued;

"With such a military machine, we need enemies constantly.

It is said that grown men are big boys with expensive toys. So is the top military brass in constant need of newer and more sophisticated weaponry and supplies. Warfare developed from stone throwing to Star Wars, and the way has been paved with faster and faster changing generations of weaponry, making the previous ones obsolete. An ancient Greek philosopher, Diogenes, was walking the streets of Athens with a lamp, pretending to be in search of Truth never to be found. He could walk now in the corridors and labyrinths of the Pentagon, with the same lamp, this time in search of military brass ready to cut its budget and give up its toys; like Truth, it will never be found.

A drastic turn of events for the military took place when the U.S. Congress passed the National Security Act, which created the Department of Defense as a layer between the Pentagon and the President. For the first time in the history of the American military, civil administrators, and politicians were on top of the Pentagon, and Congress could tighten its control over the military. This was considered a major blow to the authority vested in the top brass; authority which was taken away and given to civilians, ignorant and oblivious to the military needs and aspirations. The act has been, since its implementation, a source of numerous battles in the fields of Congress, the Senate, and in the Presidential chambers."

"So the Pentagon thinks the same way you do, that politicians are an inferior specie," I added fuel to Les' arguments.

"Actually, the frustrations and resulting bitterness and animosity have been mutual. The echelons of the Department of Defense, the Secretary included, were met with resentment, lack of cooperation, and overstepping by the top Pentagon officials. It has been very hard for battle- seasoned generals and career officers to be under the supervision and authority of political appointees, here today and gone tomorrow. More than once the Pentagon rebelled, informally, against the new boss, the Secretary of Defense, by cutting lines of information supply, ignoring newly installed procedures of cooperation between civilians and military personnel, and creating narrow loyalties different from the Department of Defense policies."

"But the President is the Main politician and the Chief Commander as well. He could interfere, if he wished," I proposed.

Les replied instantly;" Indeed, these struggles were denounced even by the only President who exchanged the military barracks for the White House, General Eisenhower. In one of his last public speeches, he warned against the dangers of the rising military-industrial power and the over spending on military projects.

This antagonism illustrated the two colliding views; the politicians claiming war is too important to leave to generals, while the military believing war is too important to leave to politicians.

Every new Secretary of Defense had come up with plans and projects to change the military, especially its budget. Sometimes, these plans were favorable for the Pentagon, but most of them were not. However, it became increasingly difficult to justify and rationalize a continuation of massive weapons buildup without having the enemies to fight against. The promises of the peace dividend, cuts in military spending, were ideal for the taxpayers fronting the bill, but bad news for the industrial concerns whose fortunes were tied in the Pentagon budget.

The new Secretary, who came at the beginning of the millennium, brought a new spirit, which sounded great, but it meant that trimming the fat is about to happen to the Pentagon. His plan of creating a lean war machine, based on outside services to be provided by contactors and subcontractors from the private sector, meant cutting into the flesh and bones of the military machine. It was a continuation of the statements made by presidents, politicians, and legislators; the Cold

War being over, there was no enemy left for which to get armed. Conclusion—cut the military budget, stop the race.

Useless to say, nobody at the Pentagon liked the plan. When the military monster does not like something or somebody, it can flex its muscles. Bad things could happen to whoever stands in its way."

Les took another brief pause.

I consulted my watch, and determining that there was more time available, signaled him to continue, which he did.

"To complete the picture, we have to add two additional elements. Wars need resources— guns and butter, weapons, and logistical supplies. The military apparatus, especially when in action, is a ferocious and uncalculated consumer of goods and services. The Middle Ages wars, when every knight brought his armor and sword to battle, have been replaced by modern warfare, requiring massive equipment and supplies. They are very costly. Their purveyors become rich and powerful and develop vested interests in military actions. The way from stone wars to Star Wars has been paved with gold for them.

When you look at most American entities involved in the supply of these goods and services, you see giant corporations with tentacles spreading into a multitude of activities, creating for them wealth beyond imagination and with an ever increasing sphere of influence. They are many, powerful and densely populated by ex-administration, ex- military, and politicians who are changing public with private service for gain. These corporations have stockholders, directors, and executives who used to be presidents, top public administrators, and military leaders, who exchanged their uniforms for business suits, and decorations for bonuses and dividends.

The last element includes the same ex-whatever, who instead of joining the private sector, preferred to act as brokers of power and influence. I mean the lobbyists."

"Excuse me," I interrupted him, "I think we are becoming too philosophical. It reminds me of the days I was invited to student meetings, where hot- blooded idealistic students used to think and talk like you are now." It was a deliberate statement, to challenge Lester to be more specific, to give me the details I needed so badly.

"You are probably right," he said. "But if you review in your mind what I've said so far, you'll get a clearer picture of the real world. Believe me; I depicted it in a very mild way. The more you know, the more you become frustrated, and then infuriated."

"Get to the point, Les," I pushed him.

"Wait just a little bit more," he answered. "We are getting close. You need to understand how high the stakes have been, and therefore, to what extremes some might go as to preserve all this."

He stopped and said; "Lets take a little break."

We walked for few minutes, quietly, each one deep in his own thoughts. We followed the perimeter set by the wall, came back to same spot were the benches were waiting for us and sat down.

A while later, he looked at me and asked; "Tell me, is the name Arthur Miller familiar to you?"

Of course it was. Trying to be funny, I answered; "Well, let's see. I had once a neighbor named Arthur Miller, but I am sure you do not refer to him. Actually, Art was nicknamed 'Miller' because of his love of beer. His best friend, Johnny, was nicknamed 'Walker,' and you can guess why."

He smiled faintly at my attempt to be witty and started talking again. "The one I meant lived and became famous when you were a small kid. He was known not only as one of Marilyn Monroe's husbands, but as a playwright and an author as well. I mention him because he wrote a short but powerful play, called *The Crucibles*. Are you familiar with it?"

"What does it have to do with us?" I asked.

"The play meant was sat in the dark Puritan period of more than two hundred years ago. However it meant to depict, actually, the atmosphere, the fear, the prejudice, and the mass hysteria our country encountered much later, in the nineteen fifties, after the Second World War, when 'communism' was the scary name to replace the 'witches' of Salem, as a result of what was called 'McCarthyism.'"

"Frankly, I still fail to see where is this leading," I said.

"As Arthur Miller said by himself, the more he knew about the Salem Witches panic, the more he saw its similarity to the McCarthy era in the fifties when the Communists were the hunted witches," Les answered.

"It is leading to a subject called 'state of fear.'

State of fear has been a very common, traditional way to control masses through the humankind history. Recently, in the last century, research has demonstrated that fear is one of if not the most powerful and effective emotions used to manipulate the public. This conclusion is of particular significance to politicians. Fear, hate and anxiety, when used skillfully, can direct the masses' feelings and decisions into almost any desired direction. As one political philosopher remarked, fear is the most effective way to rob the mind of its power to reason. He made this observation more than two hundred years ago.

Refining this method of rule and influence, the closer in time and location the object of fear is, the more powerful it is. Nobody cares that planet Earth will cease to exist in a few billion years. The melting of ice, pollution, overpopulation, and deprivation of natural resources are true issues of concern. However, it will be hard to influence the masses to take emergency actions, since they are not an immediate threat.

Moreover, fear and anxiety fade with time, as people start getting used to them. Therefore, they have to be constantly nourished and even replaced. You cannot cry 'wolf' too many times. The wolf has to replaced with a bear, a tiger, or whatever scares people."

"But what about McCarthy?" I asked.

Lester replied; "Senator McCarthy succeeded to create a mass hysteria and a witch hunt of 'Communism' in America, by inducing a state of fear. This fear, amplified through every media available, including national T.V., gave control to the F.B.I. over the lives of Americans more than ever before. Nuclear shelters were improvised, and children in schools were taught how to take cover in case of a Soviet attack. It was a period of intense suspicions directed towards whatever was or resembled Communism, including the color red. Many thousands of American citizens were accused of being members, or ex-members, or sympathizers of the Communist party and cause. They became targets of federal investigation, prosecution, and persecution by the F.B.I. These accusations and suspicions were given full credit, without any benefit of doubt and resulted in imprisonments, destroyed professional careers, and lost employment.

The media became the spreader of these hysterical fears through publicized trials and commissions investigations.

During this period, the F.B.I. doubled the number of its agents and employees and used a large variety of illegal and covert operations.

It even created a special dirty tricks menu, which included planting forged documents, disinformation through news leaked to the media, anonymous letters, and I.R.S. audits.

Now, try to replace 'radical Islam' with 'Communism,' and 'Communist' with 'terrorist.' What do you get?"

"The present," I answered without blinking.

"You are damn right. Even the federal imprisonments of McCarthy are reminiscent of the present ones held in the Federal and military prisons, such as Guantanamo Bay in Cuba, located away from the American land to avoid legal controversy."

He stopped for a moment, and then said; "Robert, I think you are getting the picture. So, let's continue one step further.

To create a state of fear, you need the right vehicle, and the vehicle is the media. Working with, influencing, and feeding the media, in this case the major T.V., newspapers, and news agencies, is of crucial importance. I think it is unnecessary to mention how the media was instrumental in instilling the state of fear in recent history and, especially, in the present.

As prophetical as the Orwellian society was, reality has exceeded, once again, the wildest imagination. Stalin was our ally in the fight against the Germans and he toasted together with President Roosevelt, and then he became our number one enemy. Saddam Hussein was our friend and ally against the Islamic Republic of Iran, and then he was transformed into our enemy. Taliban was our ally and friend in fighting to destabilize the Soviet occupation of Afghanistan, and then they became our evil and savage enemy. The same with the mujahadeen. The Soviet Union was the 'Big Evil,' the threat to our existence, and now we are friends with Russia, having cordial relationships most of the time.

The public opinion has been turned around so many times, it became dazed and confused and then indifferent. This is what is called the ultimate spinning.

When attempts were made by anyone other than the main stream and major media sources to raise questions about the variability of information fed to the public, they were discredited as unreliable, subversive, and conspiratorial.

Here we are now, when a little unknown group of unorganized fanatics, fed by the hands of a weird, but rich outcast and Saudi upper middle class idealist, became the toy of choice of the C.I.A., the F.B.I., and the Pentagon. Once the choice was made, plans started rolling and taking shape These plans transformed this small group of radicals into the symbol of evil, the newest threat to the western civilization and a dragon with numerous fire-spitting heads, all directed toward burning the American dream."

Lester noticed that his last sentences were getting close to my span of attention. He stood up, stretched, looked up at the clouds swallowing the last rays, turned to me and said;

"Now, I think we had a pretty long session today. My mouth is dry from so much talking and probably your ears are hurting for the same reason. I suggest you go on with your work today, then go home and think about what I said, because next time we meet, you better be ready for the next stage."

I did not object. However, before we reached the building, I told him;

"Listen, Les. Today I heard the most inflammatory remarks anybody could bring against his own establishment. You were right when choosing me to get into this subject, because I know you so well. Anybody else will argue with everything you say, disagree completely, look at you as a traitor or think you are completely nuts. I sincerely hope you know what you are talking about. Being in this ward and talking the way you do, you might find yourself spending in this joint more time than you wish, without even having to pretend. Your opinions will keep you here. Be careful!"

We got up, entered the building, and without saying too many words, I accompanied him to his hole.

Before entering the room, he turned towards me and asked; "When am I going to see you? I hope you haven't given up on me."

"Les, I was just about to tell you, I intend to visit you again two days from now.

Meanwhile, stay calm and don't cause any problems, please."

He smiled and, without saying anything, closed the door behind him. It locked itself automatically, separating him from the real world and its dangers, waiting for my next visit.

THIRD VISIT

We met again, as I promised both Les and my superior, two days later.

I led him out to the same spot, sat down, and shared the snacks I brought. Les, having to put up with the sparse, tasteless, and shapeless food served in the ward, considered these treats as delicacies and devoured them.

After very few words about his conditions in the joint, I encouraged him to get to the point.

Les took a deep breath and looking into the distant grey horizon, started; "The stories—the official version of the events— during and after 9/11, rather than bringing closure and verifiable truth, created more questions and doubts, not only about the incapability of our government to protect us, but about its role in the events themselves as well. In the beginning, the President objected any official and public investigations, using every excuse possible. When the White House finally gave in to the mounting public pressure and appointed a Congressional investigating Commission, the results were ridiculous. Even then, the President set conditions about the way he and the Vice President are going to testify in front of the Commission, conditions which were out of line and limited the value and validity of these testimonies.

The Commission, starting its work more than a year after the events, did not mention any facts that had not been known already. It gave unnecessarily lengthy accounts and historical narratives about the government agencies and relationships among them, which did not bring any enlightenment about what *really* happened that day. The main questions of *who*, *how*, and *why* were not satisfied and the report created even more brow-raising reactions.

Our brain and emotions refuse to accept that such evil could exist and create so many tragedies affecting so many innocent civilians just minding their own business, without any reason. But, it happened! As hard as it is to accept, we do have to accept this sad, incredible fact! And if this tragedy happened, these questions, of who, how and why, become vital for our mental sanity and peace of mind!

From the beginning, the explanations did not match the facts. Compounded by the lack of real eyewitnesses to authenticate, all were assumptions and speculations. No attackers were alive, and nobody survived the hijacked airplanes; no insiders left to tell stories.

Actually, there was one person most quoted in this report, a terrorist named Khalid Sheikh Mohammed. Apprehended much later in Pakistan, Mr. Khalid got the royal treatment from our interrogators and contracted ones. The menu of tortures offered was comprehensive, in addition to threats to kill his wife and children, sufficient to make him admit to any accusation and plot presented to him. However, these tortures made his confessions and all information coming out of him doubtful and retractable.

Basically, we have been told that the hijackings of four airplanes, their crashing into the World Trade Center and the Pentagon, and the resulting collapse of the Twin Towers, as well as Tower #7, were brought on us by a Radical Muslim terrorist organization, Al-Qaeda, created and headed by Osama Bin Laden; and it was carried out by a group of nineteen or more Middle Eastern terrorists who acquired their flight skills in private schools in the States. The hijackings were conducted with box cutters.

Whoever doubted this version has been accused of believing in 'conspiracy theories,' a derogatory classification implicating paranoia and mental instability, as well as lack of patriotism and disregard to the immense suffering and devastation inflicted on the thousands of families affected.

But what about the official story? Isn't it the ultimate 'conspiracy theory,' a story of international conspiracy, involving mysterious and shady organizations in faraway and unknown places, shady individuals and plots, with dots that do not connect? Is this official conspiracy theory more reasonable than any other?"

Les stopped for a moment, looking at me with an inquiring look.

I raised my shoulders indicating ignorance.

He kept talking; "Even before considering the conflicting facts, the main question asked is how could a group of partisans, limited in resources, on foreign ground, and in a different culture, pull such a perfect operation and of such magnitude, against the strongest, mightiest, most potent and sophisticated nation ever to exist?

Most of the Americans had never been in contact with Middle-Easterners before to be able to judge their objective limitations. To attribute to them, even if it sounds bigotry, the planning and successful implementation of such operation was more than flattering; it was an insult to the listeners' intelligence.

The typical Arab, or Radical Muslim or Middle Eastern or whatever he might be called, planning an act of terror, especially suicide missions, does it as an individual act or as part of a small unit. Remember the first nation to be hit hard by suicide terrorists. Israel. In all cases, when this maniacs succeeded and caused terrible deaths and injuries, the missions were carried by one or two suicide terrorists, very seldom more. The same in other countries, where this terrible fashion has spread; Iraq, Pakistan, Afghanistan. Every other day you hear on the news about new counts of casualties, sometimes enormous. The culprit is, usually one suicide bomber, detonating himself in public places, or using a vehicle for this purpose. Even the first attack on the Twin Towers was carried out by a few individuals. Ramzi Yousef, the mastermind of the attack, clearly stated when interrogated, that he acted with very few others, not part of any terrorist organization's plans to attack America. The attacks on the American embassies in Africa and on the ship in Yemen were conducted by teams of two or three suicide terrorists. Usually, the recruitment comes from the lowest layers of their society, where the despair outweighs the fear of death, and motor vehicles, bicycles, or their own bodies are used as carriers of the explosives. In most cases, the rumors, the field intelligence sources, and the information-for-sale would precede them. The more participants in the plots, the more chances one of them will blow the whistle. This is how the Israeli security forces have averted so many planned suicide attacks; the successful ones were carried by one or two persons.

The idea that at least nineteen suicide terrorists, backed by whatever logistical support teams and suppliers they needed, could go together through all the stages, without leaks and desertions, was ridiculous and unrealistic. Add this to their lack of knowledge of the enemy territory, and the real depth of defense lines of the opposing forces. The lack of knowledge needs to be stressed; they had no language skills, no previous exposure to Western living values, and no experience in American systems and day-to-day ways of coping with the realities of life.

Compound it by the practically unlimited resources and sophistication of the target, the American defense system. All the intelligence agencies, domestic and international, military and non-military, with the incredible array of gadgets, highly trained and educated professional cadres, pipelines of information, and policing powers, were no match for this group of terrorists. What were they busy with? The Communists? They were dead already! Other enemies just did not exist."

I had to smile at his sarcastic remark, to which he added;

"Even the rich Greek mythology, if it had to invent a God of Terrorism, could not endow Him with so many supernatural powers to be able to beat such a multi-layered and sophisticated defense system as ours."

I smiled again, but this time Les got back to his serious lecturing voice;

"The only other inevitable conclusion is, if the operation was planned and carried out by a bunch of unorganized debutants without any previous field experience; then our entire defense establishment is more than totally incompetent. It is dead. The so many hundreds of *billions* of dollars spent every single year on military, intelligence, and policing were beaten by a student project, conducted from remote caves with simple laptops and cell phones, the kind of sophisticated agencies and their state of art equipment could crack automatically and instantly.

We have so many levels of alert and counter measures, starting with overseas intelligence and borders protection and ending with Customs, the F.A.A., the F.B.I., local and state police, airport and other private security measures. Our preventative tools and measures are in space, in the air, on the ground, above and below oceans, around the world. How could they all fail, collapse, and fall simultaneously at the feet of few foreigners battling away from home?"

I shrugged again, not saying one word. He was the one to speak and he did.

"The congressional report tried to answer this basic issue by blaming it on a lack of communication and cooperation among the various government agencies. But if the average, or even above average, American brought up and educated in this society did not know about these communication problems, how could these foreigners know? How could they bet, literally, their lives on such lack of communication and coordination?

According to the official version, the hijackers used box cutters as their weapon, slashing throats and bodies on the hijacked planes. Who, when planning a sophisticated operation, would make such a choice? How hard is it to find an explanation to the fact that, if searched, a few passengers on the same flight, with similar physical characteristics and, probably, nervous behavior, had the same need to carry on-board such an unpopular tool? Box cutters are cumbersome, only a fraction of the blade protruding from its cover for the purpose of minimizing any possible human injuries. The hijackers could have used, if they wanted, a simpler means of execution, but not any less efficient, which would not attract any possible attention. They could have used electrical cords, shoe laces, belts, or even floss thread to garrote or impair their victims. This is why, when jailed, inmates are separated from their belts and shoe laces as to not cause harm to themselves or others.

But, again, there are no witnesses to tell us what *really* happened aboard those planes.

The media tried to induce us to believe there were first hand accounts. But they were not. Phone calls from planes, blinks on radar, real images of the carnage caused by this tragedy on NYC streets, conversations between the hijacked airplanes and air traffic towers, all these gave us depictions of what happened indeed and suspicions about who the culprits might be. But this is not enough evidence, or too light of evidence, when facing the gravity of the crime and the facts pointing to a different direction…

Robert, I want you to think about other facts. Ready?"

I nodded in agreement, knowing we are heading towards the target of my assignment.

Less accepted my nod and continued;

"What about previous attacks, indeed overseas, on American facilities and assets, including living quarters, embassies, and naval equipment? If they were carried out by the same enemies, as claimed, why was this enemy still alive and so efficient? We were supposed to have a military and defense system capable of fighting faraway enemies, mainly the former Soviet Union. Yet, a bunch of terrorists could attack us time and time again and we stood still and powerless.

What about previous experiences, such as airplane hijackings, in the States and overseas? We just got over the fashion of unplanned air trips to Havana, guided by your local homesick Cuban missing his family or Castro. The C.I.A. practically invented international hijacking when it became involved, successfully, in the hijacking of an airliner from a new Soviet satellite, Hungary, to the free world of Western Europe, back in the late 1940s. The Middle East terrorists pulled this stunt in almost every variation possible, successfully and unsuccessfully, for the last thirty years or more. And yet, it seems that we never learned the lesson and we did not do our homework to avoid such incidents from happening again.

Intelligence reports, from American and overseas agencies, about the possibility of further hijackings and using airplanes as weapons of destruction, kept on circulating constantly, with the same warning, 'it is going to happen!' Movies, books, and T.V. shows brought fictional versions of such events to come. Reports from the C.I.A. and other national security entities kept alerting the Administration about attacks to come. So how can we explain that not one, not two, but *four* airplanes were hijacked at the same time, on American turf, by a bunch of foreigners? Our leaders ignored these warnings! Why? Because they knew they were fabrications of organizations trying to keep themselves in business, or because of pure incompetence?

How could we be downgraded to a level below that of cave dwellers? "

The words were coming out of Les' mouth as a cascade, his eyes were burning with excitement, the veins on both temples were pulsating, his fingers massaging nervously the Diet Coke can, some spittle forming on his lips. It was obvious he truly believed whatever he was saying and reliving the events. Few times, when his voice went few octaves higher than usual, I had to motion with my hand to keep his voice down. As he was talking, his face toward me and away from the main building, I could see some motion far away, close to the entrance. I suspected that Les' behavior was monitored, and for a moment I was concerned that one of the attendants might show up to calm him down, or to protect me, or to take him back to the ward.

He kept going, jumping from one argument to another;

"This is just the very beginning of the too many questions without answers, or with unsatisfactory or laughable ones.

Let's start with the Head, the Monster, O.B.L. Who was he? Yes, please notice I am using the past tense," he said, seeing my eyebrows raising in a question mark. "I'll get to this in a moment. We all know, by now, his history and his family's fortunes. His father, Mr. Mohammed Bin Laden, was a successful businessman, building a vast construction enterprise. When he died in a plane crash, he left behind a few wives and more than fifty children, Osama included. Being close to the ruling Saudi elite, the children were given preferential treatment and fostered by these rulers, becoming part of the establishment. O.B.L. was one of many siblings, all partners to the family's treasures. When divided by such numbers, every huge fortune becomes a moderate one. So what could O.B.L.'s financial resources have been? Could they be from us, through the C.I.A. maybe?

There are no doubts about the common interests, friends, and enemies O.B.L. and the C.I.A. shared in Afghanistan, at least at the beginning of his career as a terrorist leader. While the common enemy, the Soviet Union, existed, the C.I.A. supported every terrorist taking aim at them, O.B.L. being one of them. His name became first known to us, the intelligence community, in the mid eighties, after moving to a Pakistani town bordering Afghanistan. From there, he helped fuel the Afghan war against the Soviet Union by providing fighters and resources. They were originating from the C.I.A. and Saudi Arabia through the Pakistani partners, making Mr. Bin Laden an integral part of the campaign against the Soviets. O.B.L. was a real asset for the Agency and the American interests, as long as the Communist threat existed.

No American official, no C.I.A. officer, field or headquarters, will admit any direct contact with O.B.L.

However, some facts cannot be ignored, nor erased. Osama worked directly with the Saudi intelligence services which started taking an active role in the Afghani underground war against the Soviet occupation. In a deal, reminiscent of Marshall Plan in Europe, the Saudis pledged to match all funds originating from the States, via the C.I.A. conduits, in attempt to equip the rebels with all weaponry possible.

The Saudis worked side by side with the C.I.A. and the Pakistanis. All three supporters of the Afghan rebels knew what the other two do.

The C.I.A. field officers could not, even if they wanted to, ignore the presence and the beneficial activities conducted by Osama. He acted and prospered with their blessing and encouragement. This was a period when hundreds of millions of dollars streamed yearly from the U.S.; some of these funds with the official seal of approval of Congress, some from the unused portions of the Pentagon's budgets, all being matched, equally, by the Saudi government. Any kind of weapon imaginable, from ancient Second World War to Soviet Union arms bought from its satellites, were provided to the 'freedom fighters,' the mujahadins, the same ones who became our sworn enemy a few years down the road. The lack of any organized supervision of these resources' distribution lined the pockets of many people involved with enormous unaccounted amounts.

Osama had an important role in these operations; he transferred funds from the Saudis to the arms purveyors and, as compensation, received numerous contracts for his businesses, with generous budgets and profits. These proceeds, together with the enormous profits made from purchasing arms in the international market, were channeled, later to support the newcomer into the terror groups' community, Al Qaeda."

"Are you trying to imply O.B.L. was a C.I.A. asset?" I asked, with reproach in my voice. "Maybe he was not a terrorist at all," I added with sarcasm.

"C'mon, Robert, don't you think for even a second I am that crazy, even if we are seated in a mental ward right now and I am the patient. I have no doubts whatsoever; at least as far as I am concerned, O.B.L. masterminded terrorist attacks against American targets. Whatever happened in Nairobi, Kenya, Dar al Salaam, Tanzania, and in Yemen proved the intents of Al Qaeda as it evolved in its later years. I am perfectly aware about the numerous attempts made by him and by the organization he created to harm us. However, in all these cases, teams of two or three terrorists conducted the attacks with rudimentary means, trucks or boats. In addition, African and Middle Eastern countries were closer and easier grounds to conduct terrorist activities, much easier than the sophisticated, culturally different, and well defended mainland U.S. The terrorists blended in easier and the defenses were basic or non-existent. Besides, these actions took place later, after the importance of O.B.L. as a collaborator with the West, against the Soviet Union started decreasing and then disappeared.

The shift in the way the C.I.A. treated the guy and the organization he had helped to create came after the end of the Soviet regime in Afghanistan and the complete collapse of the communist system. He was no longer needed. Not only this, but he started mingling in the internal affairs of Afghanistan, creating even more confusion for the C.I.A., which was trying to decipher the political-religious configurations changing so rapidly.

Mr. O.B.L. made some comments of unhappiness about the American continued presence in Saudi Arabia after the first war against Iraq ended. These comments created a good window of opportunity to build his image as the new American public enemy, a Radical terrorist, a threat to western civilization. Whoever was an ally till the beginning of the nineties was transformed into an enemy, an asset by itself for the agencies needing one. It was another Orwellian spin of the public, the Friend of the State becoming the Enemy of the State.

O.B.L. liked the limelight of publicity, giving lectures to jihadists and other radical Moslems, preaching in mosques, giving interviews to the international press, exposing himself to the media, and showering gifts flamboyantly. We even watched him, through the TV camera lenses, riding his horse, in a display of self confidence. He knew that public exposure is the key to leadership.

However, we Americans did more than anybody else to enhance his stature and image as the ultimate leader."

"What do you mean? What did we do ?" I asked.

"The first significant boost was given by us just before the turn of the millennium, when the base he was supposed to be staying in was attacked by a multitude of our Tomahawk rockets. We killed quite a few mujahadins, but Osama was not among them. He took off a few hours before the attack. No wonder; advance details about the coming attack streamed from the Pentagon to the Pakistanis and from them to Taliban and O.B.L. In addition, the same information was shared by us with the Saudis, reinforcing the warnings. Evidently, not everybody wanted him dead. This 'miraculous' survival made him important and invincible instantaneously and books in his praise showed up in the Middle East bazaars within a few days.

The second boost was given by us when we pointed the accusing finger at him immediately after the 9/11 events. Usually, when terrorist attacks succeed, a multitude of groups claim responsibility, basking in the international fame and exposure. O.B.L. did not even have to claim this responsibility. We threw it at him, increasing his stature in the Muslim world to unprecedented levels. We brought a lot of happiness to all our enemies, the T.V. showing them dance in the streets, ecstatic with delight at our misery. Osama had only to keep quiet and not deny the accusations, while we did the publicity job for him.

Afterwards, it became a circus. Videotapes, tapes, internet, TV; all venues were utilized to bring to the entire world every message O.B.L. supposedly wanted to relay to his enemies. Why did we play his game? Who in our Administration could be so insensitive or plain stupid, to bring all these threats in public and terrorize our people? What reason could exist other than keeping our shocked citizens in a constant state of fear, having to live with the feel of danger, dangling the evil icon in front of their eyes?

We were the best and most dedicated artistic agents, taking one person and transforming it into an idol for some and a devil for the others.

We made him famous.

You know, Robert, terrorists love exposure. A famous Middle East terrorist who had an affinity for hijacking airplanes, back in the seventies, said numerous times that hijacking one airplane gives publicity to his cause more than killing a hundred enemies.

Whenever a terrorist act takes place anywhere in the world, you get a multitude of terrorist organizations, factions or cells, claiming responsibility and victory of the cause they murder for. Only one of them might be telling the truth, maybe- everybody else lies, basking in the heat produced by the incident, hoping for their moment of glory.

One of our American counter terrorism experts compared their actions to a theatre, where every move made by the terrorists is meant to direct the spot lights to the causes they represent, the scene of the crime being the stage and the world as the audience.

In O.B.L.'s case, *we* made him the protagonist, putting him on the stage in front of millions, transforming him into the Superman of terror.

Just think, Robert, how could one person divide his time setting up and managing business enterprises, putting up an army of zealots, equipping them, and building a political and religious doctrine, in a such a short span of time, while being expelled and chased by a few governments, moving from one country to another, fighting opposing factions and competitors to the leadership of radical Islam, and taking care of his own family, which included a few wives and numerous children? All this, while being very sick."

"What do you mean?" I interrupted him again,

"O.B.L. fought with a serious kidney condition, which kept worsening, as renal diseases tend to do," Les answered back. "This kidney failure was a consequence of another health condition Mr. Osama had; he was diabetic to the point he had to inject himself with insulin several times a day. As the diabetes continued to ravage his body, O.B.L. reached the stage when he needed periodical dialysis. He was treated by many doctors, mostly Westerners, in medical facilities located, surprisingly, in Saudi Arabia and in Pakistan.

2001 was a particularly tough year for him. By July his health situation worsened to the point that he needed emergency treatments. He was in an American hospital in Pakistan, under American doctors' supervision at the beginning of September, actually on the tenth and later. A special medical team was trying to keep him alive and well, so the icon could continue to scare the West, especially the American public.

For some reason, it is hard to envision Mr. O.B.L., in a hospital gown tied in the back, in the ward prepared for him and manned by special medical teams, giving instructions to destroy the Western Culture. All this while being hooked to a dialysis machine, manufactured and operated by his enemies.

Dialysis is a delicate and complicated procedure, requiring sophisticated equipment under the most sanitary conditions to avoid infection of the blood being cleaned from its toxics.

I know this, Robert.

I am not a doctor like you, but, to my sorrow, my father passed away from kidney failure. Yes, I saw my father fight with diabetes, kidney disease and dialysis and I know first hand what a rough, physically limiting and time consuming this medical predicament is. I know also the eventual outcome.

But lets get back to Mr.Osama. As a kidney disease patient, he needed repetitive sessions in the caves of Afghanistan, in the primitive and rudimentary conditions imposed on any person fleeing from International law and from enemies such as the coalition troops, mainly ours. To survive such conditions, for any length of time, requires unlimited belief not in medical science, but in miracles.

The testimony to the lack of such a miracle is a small 'tel,' a pile of stones, in the barren wilderness of the Afghanistan mountains.

It is a burial mound.

It is an unmarked grave, its location known to a small number of people only. Underneath, as customary in the tradition of the local Muslim villagers, are the remains of O.B.L. The Afghans, more liberal in their interpretation of the religious commands, used to mark graves with colored flags. However, the disciples of Mr. O.B.L., who was the symbol of radical Islamists, with a strict interpretation of the same commands, saw the Afghans and their flag marking of burial sites as idol worshiping and did not allow such sacrilege to their leader's tomb.

It is not a place of pilgrimage, nor for prostration, in awe to the person buried there. For the locals, the guy was not Evil God, or the supreme terrorist, the ultimate martyr fighter, or whatever he would have liked to be called. He did not fight their fight. For them, he was just an eccentric, rich Arab who became a source of problems.

O.B.L. passed away in December of 2001, to the great disappointment of his American cult builders.

What a pity and unexpected setback!

America needed him! Finally, we found the ultimate evil, the scapegoat to all our problems, frustrations, and fury. His name was to correlate with the national cry for battle, but how can a dead man be used for such a purpose?

However, his body and spirit has remained with us, brought back from the dead by our miracle makers, the C.I.A. and the other intelligence agencies, through a series of videotaped interviews of poorly chosen look-alikes. It is a pity that the re-animators could not find a good match, and so far all attempts to show live pictures of O.B.L. have been pathetically amateurish.

But even these poor ear- and eye-pulling tricks could not explain how the limelight-loving leader of such a threatening, international, popular, powerful, and resourceful terrorist organization has never been seen by anybody since 2001; no rallies, no meetings, no interviews to the media, no encounters of any kind with humans.

What about some other comrades in arms of Mr. O.B.L.? Nassrallah, the leader of the Hezbollah, the Lebanese-Iranian terrorist organization, is not so shy, in spite of the Israelis just waiting around the corner to dispatch him to all the virgins promised up in the sky. It is the same with many other leaders of Arab terrorist groups in the Middle East.

If Osama Bin Laden is still alive as the public is led to believe, so powerful as depicted and ready to become a martyr anytime, why is he so afraid and lives in permanent hiding? If he is so afraid of us, why are *we* afraid of him, or of his shadow?"

I raised my eyebrows, expressing lack of appropriate answers to his rhetorical questions and he continued;

"His disciples, the nineteen or more suicide terrorists, the ones to commit the most heinous act in our history, are another good target for the arrows of skepticism. We call them the Arabs, the Radical Muslims, or the Middle Eastern terrorists. It is so typical for us to crowd the unknown into one common denominator. We, the Americans, have a common name, 'Europeans,' for the Germans who are hated by the British, for the British who are making fun of the French, the French who are making fun of the British, the Belgians who are a source of fun for the British and the French, and so on. There is no such thing as 'Europeans;' there are British, French, Dutch, German, and Polish people, all very different from each other, each nation carrying heavy baggage with hundreds of years of disagreements, differences, and disputes with their neighbors, backed by millions of dead bodies. It is hard to envision a secret pact and conspiracy being carried out successfully by such a multi-national, multi-cultural group against a homogenous entity so far away, as America would be for them. They would disagree, dispute, split, desert, betray, or sell each other way before any action would be conducted by them.

The same with our southern neighbors. They all fall into one category, 'Latinos.' Never mind their diversity and differences in culture, dialects, political structure, and other distinctive characteristics. It does not matter El Salvador and Honduras had a war because of a soccer game, or Guatemala fought with Belize trying to annex it, and only British naval presence avoided escalations. Mexico itself is a federation of fourteen states, as different from each other as Mayan Indians are from Spaniards, from the industrial north to the undeveloped and jungle abundant south. Colombians are still convinced their Spanish is the purest in the continent, and next to the politically 'emancipated' Venezuela there are still European colonies, the French and the Dutch Guyana.

The Middle East is similar in its diversity, if not worse. This is a region that has not yet reached the civic development stage of national identity as European countries have. It is still a tribal society marred by religious, cultural, sectarian, and other differences, with strong clan and tribal affiliations and loyalties.

A good expression was coined to describe these loyalties; 'My country comes before any other country, my village comes before my country, my tribe comes before my village, my clan comes before my tribe, my family comes before my clan, my brother comes before my family, I before my brother.'

According to the official version, the suicide terrorists were from a few countries on two different continents, Asia and Africa. To put together an international group with such different backgrounds and having it last through a life sacrificing assignment, no matter what the reasons and the purposes are, is a ridiculous contemplation, which just goes to show either complete ignorance or thinking that Americans are ignorant or both. The danger of internal fights and discord, amplified by the chauvinistic refusal to accept each other's authority, refusal to listen to a leader from within a group, would make any assignment impossible to achieve..."

"These are generalizations, Les," I said. "Give me some specifics, please."

"What specifics do you want?" answered Les. "Names? Everybody knows the list of the nineteen terrorists and their biographies. What surprises me is that for some reason, there are no skeptics to challenge the capability of these individuals to carry out such an operation successfully; keeping in mind they are marching to their own death.

Let's talk about the 'leader' of the group, Mohammed Atta, the Egyptian. He was an educated person, spending time in Germany. He did not like it there, although he had conducted a life considered sinful by observant Muslims. He preferred to be back home, with his two sisters and his mommy. Yes, Robert, Atta was a mommy's boy, spending time on his mom's lap way into his twenties, seeking her affection. His father kept complaining he was raising three girls, Mohammed being the third, as a result of his mother's pampering. He had to trick his only son to leave home and study in a place far away from his mom's and sisters' influence, so he could become a real man. Although everything is possible, it is very unlikely this soft, sensitive, effeminate person could go through such a metamorphosis and become the cold, calculated, cruel, unemotional person to lead a devastating and inhumane attack on innocent strangers. I envision his father smiling at the allegations about his son's crimes, taking them as a compliment to his son's manhood and as proof he could turn his son into a real man.

Another member of the group, Ziad Jarrah, was an educated person as well, born and raised in Lebanon, member of a wealthy family, and used to Western lifestyle, after moving to Germany to study. He was fond of booze, drugs, and female companions, again, not much in the spirit of a Muslim believer. He definitely does not match the profile of a suicide terrorist ready to sacrifice his life for religious or nationalistic ideals.

Other terrorist, Marwan al-Shehhi, was born and raised in the United Arab Emirates, came from a wealthy family, spent time in the military, and received higher education in a German university. Not a likely person to participate in a suicide mission to destroy the Western civilization, which had been so good to him.

Even the poorer one, Ramzi Bin Alshabib, a Yemenite, was a brilliant person who excelled in studies and got a scholarship to a German college. He was supposed to show gratitude for the extraordinary opportunity given to him by a faraway country. It housed, fed and educated him, showing him the way to enlightenment and a life better than in the remote desertuous mountains from where he came and to where he could go back whenever he chose, if life in the West was not up to his standards.

All these people, as indoctrinated as they could become with Moslem Radical beliefs, for whatever unseen reason, were not the kind to kill themselves and to carry out such atrocities.

In a way, the common denominator of these four individuals, as told by the media as part of the official story, was the disappointment and dissolution with the western values. But this is an old scenario, the one attributed to the true Egyptian father of the Muslim Brotherhood, the radical Islamic movement which started in Egypt. He was the one who supposedly came to the States to study, saw the emptiness and shallowness of the materialistic society, went back to Egypt and started preaching and fighting for a society based on the purity of the Islamic values. What I am trying to say, Robert, is that the rationalization given by us to the irrational activities of these terrorists is an old story lacking any imagination.

I am trying also to say, Robert, that it is not impossible, just extremely unlikely and unwise to put together a team comprising of an Egyptian, a Lebanese, a United Arab Emirates citizen, a person from the extreme backwards mountains of Yemen, and a bunch of Saudis. The difference in their background, dialects, family origins, education, mentality, and culture is vast. Only people completely ignorant and oblivious can ignore this fact, and assuming they brushed these differences off, to become one operational unit under the magic spells of O.B.L. and to adhere to the rigorous discipline needed to plan and carry out successfully such an operation."

Les took a brief intermission, took a sip from his Coke can, and continued; "Then there is the subject of their assimilation into the American tapestry. They lived, ate, slept, and clothed in our cities for years, coming and going and coming again, all this without attracting attention sufficient enough to try to stop them? Robert, if you went to an American Consulate in the Middle East, or any other country in the world, you'll be surprised how hard, tedious and unpleasant is the process of obtaining an entrance visa to the U.S., provided you even get one. More visas are denied than granted. You have to have sufficient financial resources, good and valid reason for the visit, and assurances you intend to return to your country. Yet no problem for these terrorists to travel freely to and from the U.S..Why?

Were the flight schools they attended just another normal, trivial activity, every Middle Easterner coming to the States engages in? No need to check, no need to take action, even if a few years back their compatriots tried to blow up the Twin Towers?

Even the congressional report acknowledged the terrorists' limitations, language difficulties, educational and cultural disadvantages, peculiar behavior, erratic patterns of domestic and international travel, and the lack of purpose for their presence in the States. This is more than enough to initiate an interest in these individuals.

But where were our protectors? If such persons are allowed to act the way they acted and carry out such an incredibly precise, coordinated, dangerous, and complicated mission, then who are the ones to be stopped? Poor Mexicans trying to cross the border? Cubans and Haitians floating to Florida?

What about the ultimate terror organization, Al-Qaeda, and in the same breath, the mujahadins and the Taliban? This is not a traditional Radical Muslim establishment born from the hate of the few privileged, ripping the riches of the area, while leaving the masses in the Middle Ages. Al-Qaeda is a newcomer to the international scene of terror organizations and we, the Americans, have a lot to do with its birth and early childhood development. It was born in the late eighties and the name says it all. It means, in Arabic, 'the base' or 'the data base.' Yes, Robert, don't look at me like I am crazy. This is not my invention. Even the British Foreign Secretary, Mr. Robin Cook, mentioned this fact to his colleagues in the Parliament."

"The only interpretation known to me," I interrupted him, "is the name was adopted because it originated in the military bases set up by the 'freedom fighters.'"

Les looked at me and said, "Robert, Al Qaeda is the name given to a computer database prepared by our intelligence agencies and, yes, mainly by the C.I.A., which included the names of thousands of mujahadins, freedom fighters. They were our allies, our weapon in the fight against Communism. These were locally mobilized volunteers and mercenaries recruited to fight the Soviets in Afghanistan and, furthermore, to shake the fundamentals of the Soviet Union by spreading the Islamic radicalism in the Muslim Soviet provinces. The fact that it became our biggest enemy and threat just comes to show how shortsighted our intelligence agencies had been.

And yet, at least in the beginning, Al Qaeda was a foreign implant on the tribal grounds of Afghanistan. Indeed, the local Pashtuns over there have a code of sanctuary, offered to any stranger knocking on their doors. However, they are needy people as well. As long as the newcomers, the Al Qaeda foreigners, mainly Arabs, provided new sources of income, they were welcome. Even then, the locals took advantage. As one of the many stories goes, the chieftain of a village sheltered a group of Al Qaeda in the village mosque. Then he stormed in telling the resting fighters the Pakistani army was almost there and they are were about to be attacked and annihilated. The chieftain urged them to leave everything behind—guns, other weapons, provisions, and even their personal belongings— and run away to hide in the surrounding mountains. It was a trick. The villagers stole everything, dividing the pilfered goods among themselves. The Arabs showed up in a close by village, some of them barefoot in the snow.

The C.I.A. did, as well, a lot to help create the mujahadin and their progenies, the Taliban, by funding educational institutions, madrasas, to teach and spread the Quran and make it the alternate ballistic weapon against the Soviets. In addition, they were provided with equipment and weapons, some to be turned against us later. For awhile in the mid eighties, this new weapon, the mujahadins, invented to bite at the heels of the Soviet empire was even put on display in front of numerous Congressional visits and other top American officials, the C.I.A. director, senators, and Congressmen included. They were shuttled back and forth to the Pakistani and the C.I.A. erected training camps, looking at the trainees with admiration appropriate for heroes ready to die for the greater cause of defending the West against the Soviet might.

The C.I.A.'s plan was a good one indeed, and the Book of Quran, printed in American funded print shops and smuggled into Soviet Republics, did more damage than anyone could imagine. The Soviet Muslims were attracted to and followed the religious radicalism like children after the sweet notes of the Pied Piper, while the old men in the Kremlin watched the march to doom helplessly. But it also ignited a fire which spread in the surrounding bushes, without being stopped till it reached the igniters and burnt us.

By the way, Robert, do you know the meaning of the word 'Taliban?'

"What is it?" I asked obligingly.

"It means 'students.' These radicals are the fruit of the madrasas, the religious schools the Saudis and C.I.A. supported. They graduated from the religion indoctrination with flying colors, becoming the most extreme fanatics our world created, except for maybe the Spanish Inquisition. They made their mission on Earth to bind not only the secular Soviet Union Muslim population to the sermons of Mohammed, but also to the entire Muslim world. However, Robert, you have to remember that we, the Americans, used to like them. As a matter of fact, we liked them to the point of inviting and hosting an official delegation of turban-wearing Taliban into our capital and into the homes of top American officials. Their sponsorship by an American oil company enhanced these relations, while they lasted. But they did not last too long. Along the way, the Taliban became more and more radical and militant, and it transformed into the other Frankenstein our establishment created, turning against the maker, the West.

What about the fifth column, the Muslim immigrants living in the States? There is no doubt that contributions and funds streamed from them to the Middle East. Charity is one of the pillars of Moslem religion; or that some of these funds ended, intentionally or unintentionally, in the hands of radicals and terrorists. But we should not forget it is common practice that immigrants, reaching a financial level of comfort, send funds to their roots, mainly to help families and charitable causes. When these funds are distributed to hands other than the ones intended it is mostly out of the control of the donors.

What about the funds and other assistance that *other* immigrant communities in the States have streamed to their countries of origin? Remember the Irish assisting fighting partitions in Ireland, Mexican illegal immigrants supporting the entire Mexican economy, the Cuban exiles in Florida flooding our Communist enemy, Cuba, with green energy in the form of dollars, and many other national minorities sending hard-earned wages and personal savings to their country of origin. They are not our enemies. They did not arrive to our shores, most of them after many efforts and sacrifices, to fight or harm us. They arrived to build a better life and to become part of us, if we would just allow them. Supporting terrorism aimed at the heart of America is like shooting themselves in the foot and jeopardizes the future of their second generation, the one to become complete Americans. To crowd the entire Moslem population into one highly profiled stereotype of terrorist supporters is a gross distortion of reality, reminiscent of McCarthy."

"Is this all?" I asked.

"No," he answered.

"Circumstantial coincidences cast additional shadows on the official story.

Think of the war games planned by the American defense system, including NORAD for the same day. For somebody trying to hijack an airplane this could have been the worst day possible, when military aircrafts are in the skies ready to fight enemies. However, for somebody wanting to simulate a hijacking or claiming that a simulation will take place, this would have been the perfect day, incorporating such a simulation in the war games.

Think of the unusual financial activities, including Wall Street manipulations of two particular airlines' stock, American and United, the same to be hijacked.

Think of the lack of flight data recorders from the doomed airplanes; they could not be found, but an intact passport belonging to one of the hijackers was found in the debris of the Twin Towers, in spite of the misadventures its carrier just went through. Data recorders, the black boxes, are equipped with a ping signal emitting device to lead searchers to their location. No pinging here. On the other hand, the likelihood of finding any paper remnants of a passport in such a catastrophic event should make the believer run and buy a lottery ticket because the chances of winning the grand prize are greater.

Think of the discrepancy between the piloting skills of the hijackers and the skills needed to fly a large aircraft and target such specific buildings at full flying speed."

Les stopped for a moment, catching his breath and wetting his dry lips with another sip of Diet Coke. Then, he turned toward me and said; "Lets talk about the weather, O.K.?"

"O.K.," I answered, not understanding what he means. However, it became very clear when he continued, with excitement in his voice;

"No terrorist could plan the *weather* on 9/11. It just so happened it was a beautiful, clear day. But it could have been a rainy, soggy morning, with low clouds or fog covering the city and obscuring the view underneath. Such mornings, when the top of Manhattan is not visible, are quite typical to N.Y.C. Nobody sane can think about a scenario where the terrorists got up in the morning, saw it is going to be a clear day, and told each other, "Okay guys, it is nice outside, we are going to be able to see the buildings from the hijacked airplanes, let's go and do it!" No! The planes had to be *directed* to the targets, rain or shine, by sophisticated guiding devices to hit the target as *precisely* as they were hit, *regardless* of weather and visibility.

The same applies to the Pentagon building, which, amazingly, was hit with astonishing precision, exactly in the part that was just reinforced, where the number of employees was reduced and the physical damage was minimal. The trajectory of whatever hit the building was so perfect, it barely touched the grass in front of the impacted section.

Think of the many reports about some of the hijackers having previous training, not in Afghanistan, but in U.S. military facilities here, on our grounds—in Florida, California, Texas, and Alabama. A few even listed a Naval Air Station as their permanent address on their driver licenses.

Think about the amazing 'recovery' of the terrorist leader's personal data. The man in charge of such a precise mission putting his most valuable possessions in luggage? 'Forgetting' personal and incriminating information in rental cars left in airport parking lots?

How could planners and carriers of such a coordinated operation be so forgetful? What is the point in packing, when headed for a suicide mission, all personal and secret stuff, such as a laptop, flight manual for a Boeing 757 and 767, simulator procedures manual, copy of the Quran, passport, international driver license, religious cassette tape, notes to hijackers, personal will, and more?

O.B.L. was on the terrorist list as the enemy of the State. Why, when the civil aviation was completely stopped after the events, were members of his family and other important Saudis flown out of the U.S.? Who was to be protected, us or the Saudis?

What about the *trillions* of dollars which the Pentagon could not answer for their whereabouts, while the possible explanations were in the documents destroyed by the attack in Tower #7?

What about the unusual flight pattern of the airliner crashing into the Pentagon? It was originally a flight pattern taking it straight into the Capitol Building when it made an unusual, amazingly difficult change of altitude and direction, an aerial maneuver almost impossible to complete even by a most experienced pilot, and crashed into a reinforced part of a building of less national significance. For a team of inexperienced hijacker-pilots, as they were determined, it made more sense and was easier to keep flying and demolish the Capitol if they wanted to achieve whatever they were supposed to achieve. This is the building portrayed on the back of every U.S. dollar, the very symbol of America and its materialistic values, not the Pentagon.

What about Flight 93 whose physical remains, fuselage or bodies, were never found and identified? The only testimony to its tragic end is a big blackened crater in the middle of a field. Have you seen T.V. reports of other airline crashes all over the world?

The grim reports show clear images of twisted, crushed, and burnt metal and body parts. Personal belongings are found scattered many miles away from the scene of the crash. Even when airplanes crash into remote parts of jungles, the middle of oceans, or faraway locations, remains of victims and debris have been recovered. Not in this case. Why?

What about the amazingly small number of passengers on each of the hijacked planes, a hidden plan to minimize the amount of casualties? This number could have been even lower. A late discovery of a cracked windshield on an earlier flight to the same destination caused a last minute shift of more than twenty unscheduled passengers to Flight 93; without them the aircraft would have been almost empty.

How can you explain the unusual high number of aerospace defense contractors, military and government employees on these flights?

There are many more unanswered questions that all point to the same direction, *away* from the official truth."

"Are you done?" I asked.

"No. Just listen," Les said animated, while trying to organize the thoughts racing through his mind. "The visual facts told a different story as well. Remember the Twin Towers collapsing with the speed of a planned implosion, the kind we have seen on T.V. so many times when old buildings are demolished in carefully planned preparations. How could buildings, which were built to withstand such an eventuality of an airplane collision, give in so easily?"

He stopped for a moment and added with pathos; "You know, Robert, even if you have not heard what I said so far, or if you disagree with me completely, the sight of the two airplanes crashing into the Twin Towers, the immediate explosion of the jet fuel *outside* the buildings, the way these towers took the initial impact without moving or collapsing partially, withstanding the kinetic trauma with flying colors, the sight of the isolated explosion flashes seen later on different floors, and then the incredibly fast implosions long after the impacts are facts not to be denied nor discarded.

If you saw the scenes when the airplanes hit the Towers, and I am sure you have seen them, like any other American, you could attest to the visual disproportion between the size of the airplane and the mass of the Towers. They looked like giants hit by a small bird, and giants don't fall from such a hit. Seeing the impact you might expect partial, localized damages, like a wound made by a small bird hitting your shoulder. But the common sense cannot accept total collapse, as if the Towers were made of match sticks, without any anchoring in the ground.

Architects involved in their planning stressed the basic guideline of isolating each floor from one another. This planning would have made the spilling of burning fuel to lower floors impossible. Among the planning parameters, earthquakes, hurricane winds, and a Boeing 707, with full fuel tanks, crashing straight into each tower were taken into consideration. Think about the big flashes of exploding airplanes that took place outside; this is where most of their fuel burnt and exploded. Not much was left to spill inside the towers and burn them. Besides, they did not burn; they collapsed in a heavy cloud of dust and debris, after small explosions could be seen, on different floors, by witnesses on the ground and by the T.V. viewers.

Even the incredible clear, perfect and complete visual documentation of the airlines' final approach and their crashes, from few angles and different cameras, pinpoints toward a premeditated and choreographed documentary, meant to show the entire world the events, without any shadow of doubt.

Think about the still unexplained imploded collapse of W.T.C. Tower #7, home of the I.R.S., the C.I.A., The Secret Service, N.Y.C. Office of Emergency Management, S.E.C. investigation offices in charge of 3000-4000 investigation files including Federal cases, Department of Defense and other Federal agencies. Not impacted by any aircraft, it had an identical end result as the Twin Towers, except it happened much later that day. A skyscraper, built of steel and concrete, just does not give in so easily and mysteriously, as a gesture of camaraderie to its giant fallen neighbors. If this was the case, the entire Manhattan could collapse if a hurricane, a small tremor or a planned demolition of an old building happens. This collapse created history twice; it was the first steel- framed skyscraper in modern history to collapse because of fire, as the official reports explained. It was also an event announced by the media before it happened. BBC and CNN had announced the collapse, in front of their viewers, before it actually occurred."

Les took a break from his furiously paced speech. He looked at the empty can of Diet Coke in his hands, crushed by his squeezes, threw it in the waste basket and returned to me, saying;

"I could keep going like this for much longer, but what for? It is more than enough to make the story given to the nation and to the entire world sound ridiculous and amateurish, insulting the intelligence and the common sense of most people."

I nodded slowly as his points started sinking in. They definitely made sense. But I had to keep getting to the main point, the purpose of my mission. I needed to try to discover what specific details and incriminating evidence Les might be hiding up his sleeve.

So I looked straight into his eyes and I asked; "Les, do you have any answers? Do you know things, events, and names that others don't?"

It was late in the game for Les to deny knowledge, if he had any. There were too many preparations and build-up. It was impossible for him to stop without reducing all previous dissertations to a bunch of meaningless words. Moreover, he cornered himself; if he stopped, his entire presentation could become a tirade of paranoid nonsense, placing him rightfully where he was, in a mental ward.

Lester kept quiet for a time, weighing the words about to come from his mouth, and after a long while, he said; "You are right. I think I know more than others and it is about time for me to share this knowledge. However, I'd like to do this another time, so let's delay it to our next date."

I told him I'll come to visit him again within the next few days.

FOURTH VISIT

As planned, I came back three days later.

I did not wish to show a lack of patience, and I needed to give him the time to put his thoughts together. My superior and instructor in the art of squeezing information out of reluctant informers told me not to take the initiative, but let Les arrive by himself to the point of wanting to talk without restraint. He said, "Indifference is your best tool in this case, Robert. Remember the priests at Catholic confessions. They just sit and let the sinners spill their guts. Trust me. I have seen it too many times. The less interest you show, the more he will want to talk."

I listened to him. I knew this would be the session I was moving toward, the one when I could possibly find out what Lester knew and others did not.

Then, the moment came.

We sat in the isolated spot in the neglected garden. The script my superior described came alive almost as predicted. After we made ourselves comfortable, finishing the sandwiches and soft drinks I had brought. I was trying to be as casual as possible, not reflecting my internal impatience, waiting for Les to start talking whenever he felt comfortable. I asked him how is life treating him in the ward and it gave him a good opening. Les started talking;

"You know, Robert, this damn place has a recreation room, where I am taken every day for an hour. I see patients playing chess or cards alone, other watching kids shows on T.V. or just staring into the void. Some of them are even funny- one guy is sitting by the window counting his fingers continuously. Each time he gets a different count, gets upset, paces around the room, then sits down and starts counting his fingers again. Another one claims to be an alien from a faraway planet, down on planet Earth for a short while, just getting ready to go back. He is very convincing and has a small group of fans, spending the recreation time around him, listening to his stories about the wonderful life on that planet. He claims to be able to take back with him one Earthling, and each one in that group is trying to gain his favors, so he could be the chosen one.

This room has a computer, and I received permission to Google for a few minutes. I used the time to read whatever I could find about this 'Parkinson law' you brought to my attention and now I know and understand more. You were so right to mention it in context of the beaurocratic apparatus of our defense organizations. Each one fits into this pattern of growing out of control, pursuit of narrow interests, lack of vision of the whole picture, ignoring the repercussions they create for the American people and the entire world. But, like I told you when you described it, they took this 'Parkinson law' to a level higher than any in the past, way beyond Mr. Parkinson wildest imagination.

You see, Robert, our defense and intelligence agencies became so big, so disproportionate to their scope of activity, that they started to fragmentize and compartmentalize. Each organization started new sprouts, and each new sprout kept its own independence and lack of communication with the other units in the same body, being in a survival mode. We have reached the stage when nobody knows exactly what we have, who is who and what is what. I by myself, who was supposed to help charter the future of the Agency, don't know its real full extent and what its all unit are…

Hey," he interrupted his lecturing mode, looking at me and then winking with his right eye," maybe you belong to one of these new sprouts that nobody else knows?"

Seeing my reaction, which tried to express how offended I was by such insinuation, he said; "Forget about it. I was just kidding."

He didn't know my heart just skipped few beats.

Then, getting back to his regular tone, he continued; "Whoever understands this law, that officials work for themselves and for each other, creating artificial justification through selfish, unnecessary, duplicate and futile tasks, and whoever understands the deep compartmentalization of our defense and intelligence systems, understands why 9/11 could happen."

He stopped talking for a while, took a sip of Coke, wiped his mouth with the back of his hands, and seemed to be putting his thoughts in order. Then, he continued;

"Robert, I promised to give specific answers. However, after you left, I debated with myself for a long time to what extent I should go. I really want to share with you all my knowledge, some of which is very specific and incriminating. But in spite of this wish, I decided to give you some answers only. I might disappoint you, but more than anything else, I want to protect you. You are too important to me and I fear that such knowledge could harm you. I have been thinking if

I should mentions names of individuals, corporations, government agencies, and any other entity I know to be specifically involved. I decided not to."

"What do you mean, Les?" I asked, trying to mask my disappointment. "What is the point of answering in general terms, when you could be specific and more convincing?" I kept pressing.

Les looked at me for awhile with penetrating eyes and said; "I believe they will be more convincing than the answers you have known so far. But I have to disclose upfront; no proofs, no concrete evidence to substantiate whatever you'll hear, other than the facts known already. These activities, resulting in the loss of so many lives and material destruction, were, undoubtedly, criminal. To bring criminal accusations, proof beyond any reasonable doubt is needed, backed by appropriate evidence. Such proof is absent, therefore, there is no point in mentioning any names. It will create vehement denials, claims of slander, and counterattacks. Evidence and documentation which could be used as proof in the courts of law have been destroyed a long time ago.

But look, this is not the first time the American public was not given the true picture, while the facts and evidence are hidden or destroyed. I can bring many cases and incidents.

The one that comes to my mind right now is the assassination of J.F.K. The fact that he was murdered could not be denied. It was done in front of eyewitnesses, the cheering crowds, same as the 9/11 events. However, the official explanation that the assassination was planned and executed by a single person, Lee Oswald, was a poor, unacceptable attempt to hide the truth. The basic facts, such as multiple gun wounds coming from different directions and the precision of the planning and the execution, contradicted this version. The killing of Oswald himself, such a short time after he was captured, eliminated the only person who could deny or admit these accusations. The congressional investigation committee was just a rubber stamp, not wanting to shed any more light on or answer the basic questions, left open-ended till our days..."

"Excuse me, Les, but my time is limited today, so lets skip the history and get more specific," I said, this time almost losing it.

"Okay, Robert, hear what I have to say," said Lester defensively, feeling the irritation in my voice. "The plan was set in motion immediately after the election of the new President in the States."

"Who set the motions?" I kept pushing.

"Who set the motions?" Les echoed me. "It is important and everybody would like to know. It is not necessary. In any organization, the Head is, or should be, the ultimate responsible person! No excuses, no apologies, no fall guys can clear the obvious responsibility of the 'main man.' No justification, no explanation can take away from the very basic fact that a President, who is given the ultimate executive authority, has to accept the commensurating, the ultimate responsibility!

It has been done in many other countries, by resigning heads of states for executive mistakes of much less magnitude, but not in America.

Our Presidents love their position and will go to every extent to keep it. How many times have we heard in the past denials and white lies coming from our Presidents? Remember the one who did not order any break-ins to steal rivals' secrets, the other who was nodding off while illegal business with terrorists was conducted under his nose and an independent nation's sovereignty was compromised, the one who told the nation to read his lips while he was saying words he did not mean, or the one who did not have sex with that lady.

The new President brought a team of senior decision makers and advisors who advocated for a smaller and more efficient Pentagon, with reduced budgets and physical resources, or in other words, less troops and weaponry. The main beneficiaries of this policy were the politicians in control of the defense budgets and the defense suppliers. The losers were the Pentagon officials, with smaller fortunes to waste. Their powers were just about to be substantially diluted. Except, these guys are tough, not to be fooled around with. It is dangerous to take toys and candies from tough guys.

The newly installed President had another serious problem; popularity. He took the throne not by a popular vote, a majority, the most basic rule of democratic systems; the decision leading to his electoral victory was actually made by a Secretary of State in one of the swing states, a state which could tilt the weight of majority of electors to either candidate. By making a controversial decision, which affected a marginal number of votes in that state, this person handed the Presidency into the hands of the less popular candidate. When her decision was contested in the Supreme Court of Law, one judge tipped the scale, affirming that decision. Bottom line, the President was chosen by the Secretary of a State and by a judge, rather than by the People. The President needed something dramatic and big to increase his popularity..."

I made a sign of impatience with my hand, to step on it and skip all these well known facts, and he switched the subject;

"At the same time, the commotion created by all the intelligence agencies, mainly the C.I.A., the F.B.I. and the Pentagon, around O.B.L. and Al Qaeda started to raise questions. It was a classical 'crying wolf' syndrome, when people who were warned too many times about a danger that does not materialize, stop listening. The doubts were about the efficiency of these organizations, the redundancy of the threats, the obsession about one single person, and the lack of determination in handling the enemy, were mounting. None of the many reports about attacks to come on us, warnings about airplanes becoming missiles directed at the heart of the U.S., and biological and nuclear weapons in the hands of terrorists had materialized.

The wolf had to bare his teeth and gnarl at the peaceful American citizens, otherwise the fear could dwindle and another iconic enemy would have to replace Mr. O.B.L. If you remember what I said in our previous meeting, the state of fear has to be freshened constantly, as to not lose the grip on the public.

By the way, Robert, maybe now is the time to mention one of the few axioms guiding me through my entire professional life."

"Which one? I know the one about accidental meetings and coincidences," I answered.

"Robert, I have another one, that might help you to digest what I am about getting into; 'reality defies the wildest imagination.' Things and events you think as impossible, illogical or improbable, might happen or had happened already. In other words, nothing is impossible," he finished. Then he stopped for a moment and added;

"I'll tell you something else; fiction has to make sense and be credible. Reality does not."

He took another sip from his can and continued;
"Signals were sent to set things in motion.
A joint team was recruited from the Pentagon, F.B.I., and C.I.A.
Everybody wanted a share of the pie, falling in grace with a new Administration. However, compartmentalization was complete, the entire operation fragmented to small operational segments; in a way, nobody could see the entire picture, except the very few top planners."

"Who were these few planners?" I tried my luck, hoping to get the answer before the defenses went up.

"Robert, don't interrupt me," he answered. "Why do you care so much about names when you don't even know what they did? Do you want me to continue?"

I nodded vigorously, concerned I pushed him too fast and too soon. "You are right," I said. "Keep on going. I am all ears."

Les slightly changed his sitting position and continued; "Teams were given specific assignments, without communication among them and no knowledge of the full scope, scale, and purpose of the operation. The plan called for an attack on American sovereignty, on American ground, sufficient to threaten the American way of life and to pinpoint international terrorism. An attack meant to cause firm reaction, showing the leadership qualities of the new President. An attack completely compartmentalized among various participants to a degree that nobody could see or understand its full scope.

The previous attacks, conducted against American interests but on foreign soil, such as military quarters in the Middle East, embassies in Africa, and loss of life and equipment in Somalia and Yemen, did not create any uproar in the States and were forgotten quickly by our complacent citizens. Something *bigger* and *closer* was needed, something spectacular, visible, and outrageous, something *nobody* could shrug off.

It called for hijacking a commercial airliner to be flown and crashed into the World Trade Center, in plain view, taking into consideration some casualties. No successful operation can be complete without casualties; it is a necessity, as much as soldiers are necessary casualties of war.

The choice of the W.T.C. was deliberate. It was not, as explained and speculated later, for what it symbolized, the Western capitalism. Manhattan could offer other choices, The Empire State Building, The

N.Y. Stock Exchange on the Wall Street, or one of the three airports. The Twin Towers had already been attacked eight years earlier. The point was made and noticed by the world, so why again? "

"Why?" I repeated him.

"The choice was based on a few criteria. First, the target had to be unobstructed, to allow the electronic equipment designed to guide the planes a clear electro-magnetic field. The location of the W.T.C. on the waterfront, with no skyscrapers close by, was perfect. Second, the design of the buildings, the metal infrastructure and the architectural novelties incorporated, promised a diminished and limited structural damage. In addition, the Twin Towers were close to a building occupied mainly by government agencies, W.T.C. #7, where a control center, headquarters for the operation, and storage facilities for materiel and supplies could be established."

"Are you implying this was an operation conducted by our government?" I asked with an alarmed voice.

"Yes," Les replied. "It was supposed to be a 'false flag' operation, one to lead and point at an enemy, real or imaginary.

Robert, these false flag operations have been on the tactical menu of so many countries, ours included, and you should stop making faces of disbelief, giving me the feeling I am, indeed, a lunatic. Do not be surprised at all by this. There are too many cases when governments or organizations conducted covert operations meant to deceive the public and induce it to believe they were done by other entities. This is a strategy of tension, to create fertile grounds for justifying hostilities against others. The Japanese used it to annex Manchuria, and few years later, to invade China. The Nazis used it to mobilize the German public opinion for war against Poland. The Soviets used it to attack Finland, and we, the Americans used it as well few times in the past.

As an example for a more recent one, let me mention one case, an operation called 'Northwood,' initiated by the Pentagon and presented to the Kennedy administration by the Joint Chief of Staff. It called for crashing an American airplane and sinking a Navy battle ship in the Cuban waters, as pretext for reprisals against Castro. The plan even included details about a mock list of American casualties and staging their burial. This plan was never activated, but it showed what the Pentagon could come up with."

Les took a small pause, taking another sip from the Coke can his hands were playing with, and continued; "Lets get to the main subject.

Although the results of 9/11 were so devastating, originally the top planners did not anticipate anything else other than a big flash in the pan with relatively low casualties—what a big mistake."

"Why?" I asked.

Les answered, "There were a few previous similar incidents which illustrated that the body count could be very low.

One event happened not far away, in Manhattan itself. On a foggy day in July of 1945, a U.S. bomber took off from Newark. Flying at a low altitude, in the soupy skies, it crashed at full speed into the tallest building on the island, the Empire State Building. It was a B25 manned by three crew members who flew it straight into the seventy-ninth floor of the building. The fuel tanks were full, as the plane did not have time to use much of it. The impact resulted in the explosion of the fuel tanks, and then the plane itself. One of the engines went through the entire floor, exiting the building and landing on top of another, lower building. Another engine entered the building and, landing on top of an elevator, descended together. Final tab: four floors damaged and eleven people, inside and outside the building, including the crew, were killed; a relatively low number of casualties and limited structural damages, but with tremendous exposure. The fuel tanks, exploding first outside at the point of impact, created a very visible and dramatic effect. The fire and the smoke, said the stories from the witnesses, amplified by the traditional fear of flying, made one great scenario.

Another incident brought the same conclusions. On the evening of October, 4 1992, Israeli El Al Flight 1862, a 747 Boeing freighter with a wing span of 212 feet and weight close to 700,000 pounds, just left Scihphol Amsterdam Airport in Holland, destination Tel Aviv, when it developed engine problems. The pilot called the traffic control tower within minutes of take off, declaring a Mayday situation, imminent disaster. The conversation lasted about ten minutes and ended when the freight aircraft crashing into the middle section of a nine story residential building, part of a suburban complex close to the airport.

In spite of the enormous quantity of jet fuel, meant to last at least five hours of flight for a jumbo jet, the damages were substantially less than feared. Only the section of the building which was directly hit burnt from the spilled fuel, burned and collapsed, without total collapse of the remainder of the building. The crash happened after 6:00 p.m. when most of the families were at home, yet less than forty people, inside and outside, were killed. A big hospital close by, after receiving information about the crash, prepared one hundred and sixty beds, anticipating major casualties and injuries; only twenty-seven wounded patients arrived. Again, it was a spectacular incident with tremendous fire and smoke effects, resulting in relatively minor casualties and physical damage."

I signaled Les to stop, needing to stretch for a moment. I also wanted to scroll in my memory the associations this last incident brought.

Then I remembered. The accident created a lot of controversial stories. They started the night of the crash when, according to numerous eyewitnesses, mysterious men in white and yellow protective gear descended from helicopters and started digging, poking, and searching the smoldering rubble. The area was cordoned and access was restricted while these persons were conducting their activities. Something special and important was in the cargo and attempts were made to recover it with outmost urgency.

Afterward, complaints started piling up, coming from the residents in the immediate vicinity of the crash. These were health complaints and issues serious enough to cause a Dutch parliamentary investigation into the circumstances and the cargo contents of that ill fated El Al flight. This investigation, followed by another parliamentary one, of the Israeli Knesset, concentrated on the secret chemicals transported by the aircraft. The flight itself originated in N.Y.C.. Amsterdam was just a refueling stop. Its cargo contained chemicals purchased from an East Coast manufacturer, their final destination being an Israeli government agency. Rumors, speculations and allegations floated around about the poisonous nature and effects of these chemicals. I did not clearly remember the final outcome other than some admissions in this spirit and the compensations showered on the health affected Dutch. In any case, the cargo of the plane had nothing to do with the point Les was trying to make, so I did not bring it up.

Few moments later I sat down, waiting for Les to continue, which he did; "The expectations were that when an aircraft would crash into one of the Twin Towers most of the fuel exploded outside, while the special structural design of the building would protect it and its occupants from substantial harm. To minimize the number of casualties, the time picked for the final impact was before 9:00 a.m., when most of the buildings were still expecting the waves of incoming employees and before the streets below crowded with tourists and passersby's. Remember, Robert, the area around the Twin Towers does not have as many hotels as other areas of Manhattan. People come at 9:00 a.m. or later and leave in the evening. If the hijackers wanted to maximize the number of casualties, they could have accomplished that one or two hours later or by choosing a more populated part of the city.

It was supposed to be just a big flash up in the sky and some casualties to enhance the drama, to get the needed national and international exposure.

He made a brief pause, and then looking into my eyes said; "Robert, please put this in the right perspective. What are a few lives when the national interest is at stake? There are no wars without casualties. This was a different war, but still one, so loss of life had to be taken into consideration and even hoped for. Otherwise, the whole operation would have been futile.

The disaster was a direct result of an operation carried by rival teams, fragmented into small sections and compartmentalized without having knowledge of the whole picture, without communication among them, and by gross misjudgments of the very few ones who knew all.

One big mistake, another blotched operation.

The hijacking had to be associated with international terrorism. For this purpose, the plan called for the utilization of human assets, Middle Easterners under the control of the C.I.A. and the Pentagon. These assets, individuals under employment contracts with U.S. agencies, had been trained, supported, and given freedom of living in the States as well as traveling whenever and wherever they desired.

The Pentagon and C.I.A. has had quite a big list and choices that had to be made.

The only problem was it was very hard, if not impossible, to convince these individuals to pay with their lives for the benefits received. They were mercenaries, not suicidal. They enjoyed life and celebrated it, sometimes in bars, lounges, and casinos chasing loose women, in complete contradiction to the rules of Quran and the religion for which they were supposed to sacrifice themselves. The last thing they wanted was to die.

Knowing their possible fate, no one could be found and relied upon, willing to kill himself for the sake of his employer.

Due to the low level of esteem the controllers had for these contractors and their reliability, back up and fall back plans had to be put into place in case the first attempt failed, as it had happened in many instances before. So, instead of hijacking one airliner, two would have the same fate. In case one attempt failed, it would be followed instantly by another.

A story, a convincing one, had to be told to induce them to participate willingly. The one formed and disbursed among these teams of operators, later to be called suicide terrorists; it is a simulated, staged, hijack of a commercial airliner within the frame of the war games played by the military that day, in total coordination with NORAD, the North America Aerospace Defense. In order to create a sense of real danger, they had to pass as Middle Eastern terrorist hijackers, simulating the entire process, from airport clearances to 'overtaking' the crew and the passengers. The pilots and the cabin crew were told as well that a simulated hijacking would take place and they had to play their role as naturally as possible to authenticate the simulation.

Nobody, pilots included, was told they were marching to their death.

One of the leading military aerospace defense contractors, specializing in electronics and avionics, was assigned to create a beacon guidance system similar to the ones used by commercial airports. The systems have been in use for many years and were the main facilitator to instrument landings in bad weather and poor visibility. New sophisticated versions, called Joint Precision and Landing Systems, had been completed and tested successfully. The guidance systems designed for this purpose could disengage the automatic flight pilot, take over human commands, and guide the plane to the designated spot. These systems were installed in the upper floors of the Twin Towers, and they had the task of bringing the planes home, into the Towers…"

"Excuse me," I interrupted, "How could these systems, or equipment, be brought to the upper floors without somebody noticing the suspicious activities. Are people blind? Were the Towers without any security personnel?"

Les answered quickly; "You are absolutely correct to ask these questions. Indeed, for a few weeks prior to 9/11, numerous complaints and reports were filed about such activities. The answer given was that they were part of security simulations conducted by WTC management. The equipment itself was installed on floors vacant of tenants. However, people working below and above these floors kept complaining about the continuous unexplained noises and disturbances."

He stopped for a moment to let his words sink in and continued; "Not leaving any incriminating evidence was the most essential part. To explain the presence of such systems in the buildings if the operation succeeded would be embarrassing, and to remove them after the fact would be impossible. This evidence had to be destroyed and it had to be done on the premises. The team from the defense contractor in charge of designing and installing the systems, which occupied a shared office on one of the highest floors of W.T.C. #2, was evacuated just prior to the events, possibly in anticipation of events to come. By the way, with their headquarters being located in California, a few of them ended up as passengers in the hijacked planes, assuring their secrets would go to grave together with them.

The floors, in both towers, containing the system and all the supporting equipment had to disappear to bury the evidence. Explosives were placed on these floors, calculations being made for the destruction of a few of the floors only.

Nobody could anticipate any major structural damage, especially having the explosives placed on higher floors. The demolition team did not know that airplanes carrying vast quantities of fuel would crash into these buildings. They did not know a disastrous combination was just about to be created between their explosives, the kinetic forces of the impact, and, literally, the added fuel to the fire.

The plan was approved, refined into fragmented operational details and operating instructions assigned to different teams, mainly from the C.I.A., Pentagon, as well as JSOC.."

Lester stopped, looking at me with anticipation in his eyes, wondering if I knew what 'JSOC' means. I didn't want to disappoint him, to show lack of interest, or, even worse, to indicate I might know the meaning.

So, I asked him; "Who is 'Jaysee?'

"Robert, this is not a person, it is an organization. The letters JSOC stand for Joint Special Operations Command; the joint headquarters for studying special operations requirements, for planning and conducting joint special operations and training and developing joint special operations tactics. It is a highly classified organization that coordinates Delta Force, Navy's Seals and other highly trained units. This body, which was born after, and as a result of President Carter's failed mission to save the Iranian hostages, has conducted highly classified operations and activities domestically and overseas."

"But didn't you mention the Pentagon? Delta Force and the Navy Seals are the Military!" I dared to venture.

Les answered; " The Command operates in parallel to the Pentagon and, in a way, it is its surrogate. It does not take orders from the brass. It has developed a direct chain of command with the top Administration, the very top, taking orders and reporting directly to it, without the need to go through the military chain of command. It is autonomous, independent and flexible for quick action. Even the Pentagon and the C.I.A. don't always know what they are doing. It is way over their head…"

He stopped for a moment and said; "Here we go again. You make me say things I should keep for myself, for your own sake. Stop squeezing stuff you should not know. I am glad I stopped just in time."

Lester composed himself and returned to his regular narrative tone;

"This is when the plan fell into the hands of another inside group with other interests.

The group, consisting of career top brass, believed the political system was a corrupt one, endangering the strength and the supremacy of the U.S. as the world's leader by weakening the military. All politicians, starting with presidential candidates and down to Congressmen, have incorporated tax cuts into their campaigns. The most favorite target for budget cuts, when lacking enemies to the national security, has been the military, the Pentagon.

These politicians had already created damages and they were about to cause additional ones.

They had to be stopped.

They had to be replaced with people of vision who could see the historic role given to this country to lead the world.

The problem was that all candidates with such vision had to first be elected, and in order to be elected, they had to make same promises, such as less taxes, cutting federal budgets.

Back to square one.

Politicians were not the answer.

A new order was needed, one in which the Pentagon was the leader and the President, chosen by a political process, would be more of an honorary status, as in many other countries. The timing was good for them.

The new President, with no charisma and no heroics, started his first term off on the wrong foot, fighting and justifying his own credibility and acceptability. He, like his father, a previous President, had promised to cut taxes and directed the knife to the military budget, as a benefit of the world peace. Moreover, not being directly involved in previous national politics and power struggles, he had to rely heavily on his team of politicians and advisors, veterans of previous Administrations, who were experienced in the inroads of Washington. These close advisors had one thing in common, belief in a leaner, more efficient military machine, shifting resources and power to civilian contractors.

A whole presidential term, or God forbid two, could have had disastrous effects on the Pentagon. This President was influenced heavily by his father. The former President stopped the first war in Iraq instead of going in, conquering the country, and perpetuating the war, as the Pentagon pleaded. He had a simple exit strategy; don't go in! The son could be the same, dangerous for the wellbeing of the military.

Even the number of the armed forces could be reduced. A new domestic army of mercenaries started developing already, its creator from Minnesota erecting training camps in South Carolina and starting to take away from the responsibilities of the armed forces. Their special Elite forces have been already active in many countries, doing the needed dirty jobs without having to wait for the Congress approval.

They were contractors, taking orders from their employer, not from politicians or beaurocrats.

The Vice President, a veteran of the Administration as former Secretary of Defense, nominated his old buddy, a former Chief of Staff in a previous Administration, as the new Secretary of Defense. Both of them were on the Pentagon hit list, unwanted, dangerous for their strong advocacy for a leaner military and cutting the Pentagon budget, stressing the need for more efficiency.

The defense contractors, starving for lucrative contracts, were imposing a lot of pressure for new ones. Something had to be done and the sooner, the better.

The plan to hijack commercial aircrafts and to crash them into buildings that were symbols of the nation was expanded. An exact duplication was to take place, except the target would be even more symbolical. What can be more challenging than having your military headquarters attacked at the same time by same enemies?

Like the Twin Towers, the open space surrounding the Pentagon enabled installation of guidance beacons for the incoming plane without any field obstruction. Then, when the nation was attacked, the military would assume command and overrule the politically induced and watered down presidential and Administration acts and reactions. It would be assisted by a shadow government, in the same fashion as the plans for national emergency, which called for the continuity through a shadow government.

"What shadows are you talking about?" I asked.

He answered; "Plans were in existence since the heydays of the Cold War for an emergency shadow government as an alternative, in case the top Administration officials fell as casualties to a nuclear attack. The planned shadow emergency government had some of the regular branches, but with all of them reporting to the highest authority, the military."

"Wait a second," I jumped in. "You are heading in a dangerous direction and weird one as well."

He looked at me, made a calming motion with his hand, and said; "This idea, as daring, outrageous, and far out as you think it is and as it appeared to be when first articulated, was not even an original one. It was not the first time the White House and our political system was threatened from the inside. It happened before and not in the distant past. Let me tell you about a similar situation.

1933 was a rough year for the American people. The great depression caused much bitterness and raised questions about the validity of the political system, one that brought hunger and desperation to millions. In this atmosphere, a group of influential business people, including industrialists, bankers, and the media elite, conspired to undermine the powers given by the People to the new President, F.D. Roosevelt, and place a military person to 'relieve' the President from most of his authorities.

The person chosen to head the coup was a retired Marine, Major General Smedley Butler.

It could have been a good choice.

The guy was extremely popular, especially within the ranks of the veterans. Decorated numerous times, the Major General, nicknamed 'the fighting Quaker,' had clout and followers.

The plan was to induce and mobilize the veterans of WWI, more than 500,000 of them, and transform the American Legion into an army, requiring power for Mr. Butler. In a way, it was a repeat of what had been accomplished already by Hitler and Mussolini, who took the reigns of their countries with the help of unemployed, starving, and bitter veterans of the same war. However, the attempt to overthrow, or neutralize, the President failed. The failure was due to a simple reason; the conspirators chose the wrong person. The Major General, faithful to his oath, blew the whistle.

His discoveries led to a Congressional investigation, the McCormack-Dickstein Committee, which issued a report. It confirmed the Committee received evidence showing certain persons had made an attempt to establish a fascist government in the U.S. It also confirmed such attempts were discussed, planned, and might have been placed in execution when and if the financial backers deemed appropriate. No actions against the conspirers were taken, and in the American history books, this episode did not get any mention. Among the reasons given for the hushing and downplaying of this coup attempt was the control over the existing limited media, the newspapers, by the conspirers themselves.

Another reason was a deal made by the President himself. F.D.R. had one target, to pass his economical revival plan through the political hoops. The plotters walked away free and without public embarrassment in exchange of the support of Wall Street and the other industry moguls for the New Deal and the President."

Looking at me, he said; "Robert, this might give you a new insight into the meaning of the expression 'the New Deal.' This episode, so little known by our public, is just one example. In a way, every assassination of an American President, or attempt to, should not be considered a personal attack, but an attack on the whole system, ideas, and actions these Presidents represented, Lincoln and J.F.K. included."

Then turning his eyes into the distance, Les went back to the subject; "The plan to attack the W.T.C. was a disastrous one, full of failures and mistakes, greed and profiteering. The demolition team was kept in dark. They did not know airplanes with full fuel tanks were about to crash. Their assignment was specific: detonate certain floors, put enough explosives to pulverize whatever was inside, and rely on the structural integrity of each floor. However, the combination of the physical trauma to the structures, accompanied by leftovers of airline fuel spilling inside, amplified the effects of the carefully placed explosives.

The buildings did not collapse when they were hit. They fell after the detonation of the explosives. What was supposed to be a sequence of isolated explosions, muffled by the raging inferno outside and attributed to the spilled jet fuel, became a total unplanned, unexpected, and unintended catastrophe.

The tragedy was doubled.

The second crash was not needed anymore, but it was too late to stop it. The contact with the second aircraft ceased to exist, its controls debilitated, and the guidance system, installed in the Tower kept bringing in its subject, straight into the upper floors.

W.T.C. #7 had been the nerve center for the entire operation, a storage place for equipment and materiel. Largely occupied by Federal agencies, its premises were requested for this operation. The magnitude of devastation called for an immediate and complete erasure of anything which could be found and point to the culprits. There was no time for systematic cleansing, floor by floor, each desk and drawer. Everything had to go and fast. Indeed, everything disappeared many hours later on this tragic day. For no apparent reason, the building gave in to the same fate, a careful imploded collapse leveling it completely. The whole world watched it happen and nobody could explain why and how.

The ones who knew what was about to happen and knew how to do it, took financial advantage from the events about to unfold. Bets were placed on the floor of the biggest casino in the world, the Wall Street Stock Exchange, on a dramatic drop in the value of the airlines subjected to the hijacking, an inevitable outcome of the crashes. It was a safe bet, knowing the outcome. However, the results being so devastating, nobody wanted to attract unnecessary attention by cashing in the prize, and most of these gains remained unclaimed or the beneficiaries remained completely anonymous. Tremendous quantities of gold ingots, stored in the vaults of the Twin Towers, disappeared, their destiny still unknown. Yes, there were ways to make the best out of the worst and some people did just that.

The simultaneous plan in D.C. was a complete success. The first attempt to attack succeeded. The Pentagon building was attacked, resulting in limited structural damages and a relatively small number of casualties. Remember, Robert, this operation was planned and carried out by a unified military team, coordinated and organized. The results were as expected, without glitches.

The back-up plane was not needed anymore.

The aircraft was successfully stopped in midair, by unknown means, and the only testimony to its dramatic fate was a huge crater in a remote field.

There was no further need for additional damages. The point was made, and the whole world took notice.

The road to action opened.

The President was not visible.

His plane took off and nobody knew where he was, except that he was circling the skies, running away and hiding. Hours and hours passed and the shell shocked Americans kept asking, "Where is our President?"

It was a great way to display leadership qualities befitted to a Commander in Chief.

But it was not really his fault.

He was a hostage of the military.

His airplane, after taking off abruptly from a Florida airport, was escorted by military fighter jets, for protection supposedly, to a military Strategic Command Center, where conditions were presented for his return to Washington.

The V.P. was at an undisclosed location. He was held against his will as well. His doctrine of a leaner military machine and budget cuts had to be changed to a hawkish, aggressive policy, wars and military actions.

The President and his Vice President were not free people. Conditions were put in place for their return; obeying the Pentagon rules.

The plans for the shadow emergency government were pulled out. They included a narrow body of less than one hundred and fifty officials, chosen to keep the continuity of the government under military protection, in secret undisclosed locations. Military actions, increased military spending, declarations of war, free hands to activities unheard of before, and limitations of freedom rights were part of a new order where the Pentagon dictates what and when. The alternative presented to them was simple and straightforward; their replacement with the shadow emergency government, or return to the White House and put the Administration under the Pentagon, not above it.

The coup which failed in the thirties succeeded seventy years later.

The President made the deal, this time as a loser. When the chief executives are hostages, choices are limited.

When he returned to his palace, the President was a beaten man and so was his close entourage.

Whatever was preached before, changed, and the changes were immediate and radical. The Pentagon won, and the winning was big, as a reality check down the road can show: two wars, immense military spending, assumption of emergency powers, declaration of national emergency, limitations of freedom rights, and all other signs characterizing a militaristic environment taking over a political system.

Many of the participants in the specific phases of the operations perished in the events, minimizing the danger of leaks; some were in the crashed planes, some in the wreckages of the W.T.C., and some disappeared shortly after. The ones left were safe. Nobody in his or her right mind would divulge any connection, directly or indirectly, with these events considering their outcome.

Here we are, a few years down the road, when Americans forget what complete freedom and respect of human rights means.

We even got used to thinking in terms of 'before' and 'after' 9/11, in terms of personal freedom—all in the name of national security.

Almost every day brings news about infringements on our freedom and abuses by the Administration.

However, they are not by choice.

It has to be done to keep the end of the bargain, putting the Military in the driver seat.

Mass communication tools have been displaying alert color codes telling us when to bury our heads in the sand, new 'plots' are 'discovered' and 'foiled,' airports have become the scene of human degradation, security cameras follow you wherever you go, the holy principles of privacy have been abandoned, the country is depleting its riches, wasting them on guns instead of butter, families are burying their dead and caring for the wounded and maimed, but the Pentagon has a feast."

His last sentences left a somber atmosphere.

Lester stopped for a moment, feeling the effects of his words, and then said, with attempted humor in his voice, trying to break the silence;

"You know, Robert, after I missed a flight because I was singled out and searched thoroughly by the airport security, I was thinking that if I have to travel, the best alternative is to use a Middle East airline. Who knows, maybe my next trip will be with Royal Jordanian Airline or Lebanon Middle East Air. Nobody on these airlines will make me drop my shoes and get undress in front of others to see if I carry weapons or chemicals."

I looked at Les, smiled at his attempt to diffuse the tension created by his speech and said; "Let me try to summarize what you stated, to make sure I understand you correctly; the 9/11 events were planned and carried by our government as a false flag operation. It was supposed to be, originally, a spectacular display of smoke and fire with few casualties, meant to direct the public attention to a new, dangerous enemy that replaced the defunct communism threat. However, due to mistakes, complete compartmentalization, miscalculations and gross misjudgment it became an unplanned major national disaster, later to be exploited to increase the power and the influence of the military. Is it correct?"

"Yes," he answered."

I let him rest for awhile, and then I asked; "Is this all? It sounds very convincing, but can you give me some more specific details, names, places, something to demonstrate that whatever you said is not just another conspiracy theory?"

Les looked at me and said with a tired voice; "No, Robert, I cannot and I will not. Such knowledge will put you in the same danger I feel I am in; your life could be in jeopardy.

You are absolutely right. Without hard evidence, names, firsthand testimonies, and documents to prove what I told you, it is just another conspiracy theory."

He stopped for a while, and then continued;

"Let me add just another ingredient to this story; the reason I am here.

I started asking questions.

I inquired. I tried to access sources of information that were open to me before. But starting to poke into the details of the operation, doors began shutting in front of my nose. A reorganization pretext took away my top secret clearance, leaving me with one fit for a junior clerk. Then funny things started happening around me.

I felt like I was shadowed. The house across from mine, which stood vacant for a very long time, was rented overnight to two young, well built gentlemen. They are not the kind of tenants somebody would expect in such a large suburban home. They watch my house and me. They keep coming and going, but one is always there, on duty.

My mail was arriving resealed. Somebody read it before me.

My computer was acting funny. It was tampered with.

My land line was tapped, and I could sometimes hear the breathing of the listener.

There was no subtlety in these attempts. It's like I was being deliberately told;

'Watch it! You are being watched!'

I know it sounds like a classical case of paranoia, and this is exactly what my wife told me when I shared my fears with her. 'Your job got into your head,' she said. 'This is what happens to people who spy on others, like you did all your life.'

I started hearing about unexplained deaths of people I knew as being associated with the operation. Others just disappeared. I felt I was in danger. I did not know where to turn. Then my wife's words gave me the right idea; if I am crazy, I should be in a mental institution. This is one of the very few places nobody can access and harm me. In the company of Jesus, Napoleons, God himself, and other loonies, who would pay attention to a person dreaming about some imaginary conspiracies?"

While Lester was saying this, I kept thinking to myself, 'Les, if you only knew! We found you already!' I hoped my face did not divulge my thoughts and Les continued;

"I made my final decision a few weeks ago. I had just gotten out of my car, in front of the house, to pick the newspaper. A little kid from the neighborhood came to me and gave me a little piece of paper. I tried to get out of the kid who gave him the paper, but the only thing he could say was that he was an older white man, without a beard, but maybe with a little moustache. But he was a nice person. He gave the kid five bucks for the errand.

Evidently, it must have been one of the very few friends left, after so many years, in the Company, who wanted to warn me without risking his neck. Rolled in the paper were a few words cut from a book, numbers on their back. I put the words in numerical sequence and I got my final warning. It was one sentence, "You have reservations overseas."

I knew what it meant.

I was about to be dispatched to one of the detainees camps, set up by our government in one of the few European countries hungry for our dollars. It was the new way America discovered to torture and conduct other clandestine and illegal activities; hidden away from the eyes of the public, in other countries, with subcontracted services. Money streamed from our government and back came a stream of constant information, literally squeezed out. In these camps, political prisoners, suspected terrorists, and other enemies of the state were interrogated. The methods used were not pleasant; water boarding, electrical shocks, truth drugs, and any kind of mental torture developed by professionals as not to leave physical scars.

The mental ones were a different story, as you can imagine…

Look at me, I am still here and still alive. But, believe me, Robert, it is not easy being in a loony hole. The other day I saw a patient removing a fire extinguisher from its place. I don't know what he intended to do with it, but, evidently, the attendants knew. They cornered him and started beating him till he was full of blood. Afterward, I started paying more attention and noticed many patients with blood on them. I could tell you, Robert, as you probably know and remember, I have seen a lot in my life. But I have never seen such a bunch of tough and vicious people as the mental ward attendants are. They are treating patients like rabid animals, there is no mercy left in them. They are, however, my protectors. Nobody can penetrate through them. Even a judge's order to get me out will be ignored, unless supported by medical recommendation. The liabilities in releasing a lunatic into the streets are higher than releasing a regular criminal. A lunatic is more dangerous.

In the short period I have spent here, I have seen so many crazy people I miss the normal world. I never knew there could be such a large collection of rapists, axe murderers, sex offenders, and other violent people keeping each other company, under the supervising eyes of professional handlers. These are people who have been in and out of institutions like this all their life, arguing and talking loudly to God, the Devil, or Presidents as they were their best friends or worst enemies. This mental asylum has become my political asylum, but it's started taking its toll on me."

He stopped, caught his breath, and then looking straight into my eyes, said;

"Robert, the past few days I have been thinking I could not last much longer in this hole. I came in as a completely sane person, but I am afraid to turn into one of those mental cases, just by the virtue of being here. Nothing can make you crazier than being under lock and barrel in a public mental ward. Just wait till you are in a place like this, where insanity hits your face wherever you turn.

The funniest thing is that every patient here tries to act normal and sane, so he or she can get out. Only I have to act crazy, in order to stay in."

He stopped for a moment, and then he said with a plea in his eyes; "I need your help." Seeing the puzzled expression on my face, he added; "I want you to get me out of here and to a safe place, where nobody can trace me. I truly believe that the only one who can save me is you. I don't think I have to elaborate any further.

Will you help me?"

I avoided his eyes. I looked into the void for a while, thinking, got up, and answered; "Lester, I'll do my best. Just hold on a few more days. I need to think how to do it. I owe you my life and the time has come for payback."

No more words were needed.

I accompanied him back to his shelter and then left the premises.

On the way to the car, I made up my mind.

In the parking lot, I removed the recording device which absorbed every word said, rewinded the last few minutes of our conversation, and replaced our voices with the screeching noise of a subway stopping in the nearby station.

When I arrived to my office, I called in my special assistant for this project and threw the tape at him. He caught it in the air, smiling at me with the trophy in his hands.

Then he asked; "Get anything good out of it?"

"I doubt it," I said. "This guy is completely off the tracks. He really belongs where he is. But, listen to it and write down every word in a memo. Frankly, I think it was a complete waste of time—no names, no hidden documents, nothing new.

Just a lot of blah blah."

When I received the transcript, I sent it to my boss, together with my comments:

JUST ANOTHER CONSPIRACY THEORY.

I RECOMMEND TO CLOSE THE FILE.

A few days later the name Lester Ross was taken off the list of assignments.

LAST VISIT

Lester was no longer in danger, at least not from his former employers. However, he was undesired as an employee. His institutionalization in a mental hospital was an official, satisfactory reason for dismissal from his duties. A letter sent to his home informed him about his forced retirement due to health reasons, accompanied by generous benefits.

I could not tell him I knew all this.

I could not tell him I have been employed by the same Company; indeed, in a completely different capacity and scope of activity.

I could not tell him I agreed to take the assignment to spy on him.

I knew the letter of termination would not convince him he was safe, but was possibly another trap to get him out of hiding, to smoke him out.

Maybe it was.

He needed my help, and I had to do it his way, as an escape.

A few days later, I arrived to his temporary asylum equipped with all documentation required to officially release him from the mental hospital. The waiting room attendant, who knew me and my subject of interest by now, gave me a faint smile of recognition. I took him into his small office for a conference. I got straight to the point;

"Mr. Ross needs to get out, but he refuses. You know how paranoid and schizophrenic he is," I added. "His family wants to transfer him to a private institution, where he can receive more personal attention and treatment, even if it is going to create a big hole in their budget. Hey, if this is what they want, they have the right to do it," I continued.

Then I explained to make Lester's exit off the premises easier, he had to help me stage his exit as an escape. The attendant already knew the patient had paranoia and was looking behind his back constantly, so my request sounded reasonable.

We arranged a scenario that when he saw Les and me approaching the waiting room, he would get out for a short while and leave the exit doors unlocked. We would follow and get out of the building, and then he could get back to his duties.

"I already made the arrangements for the intake at the new facility," I told him, while showing him briefly papers with a private hospital logo containing the name Lester Ross.

He obliged.

When I entered Lester's room, I put a finger on my lips signal the need to keep quiet. I gave him the little package with some clothes in what I estimated to be his size.

He changed quickly and the old Les I remembered reappeared, replacing the public ward inpatient. We quietly left his room and followed the hallway to the waiting room.

The attendant, seeing us from far away, turned his back casually, got up, stretched lazily, and left the building, while shouting over his shoulder to an invisible attendant, "I am going to get something out of my car. Leave the doors open, I'll be right back."

Good show! He really got into his role very well.

We followed.

In less than five minutes we had crossed all obstacles and were seated in my car, this time my own, not the one supplied by my employer.

I explained to him the rest of the escape plan and he agreed.

After pulling into a gas station, Les went into the men's room, used the toiletries I had bought for him, and a few minutes later came back clean shaven, his hair combed and looking groomed. What a difference some grooming and a good shave could make! He looked younger and healthier.

We started a three day driving trip to the southwest corner of the country.

We drove south on I-95, then I-85 to Charlotte, N.C. There we turned west on I-40, crossing the entire width of Tennessee. The first night found us in a road motel off the highway in Arkansas. The second day, we kept driving due west, still on the same interstate. Fourteen hours later, we found another sleeping hole, this time in Arizona. The third day we spent crossing the state. It is one big state, especially when you drive through it all by yourself. Lester never touched the steering wheel. He did not want to take the chance of being stopped by the highway patrol for any possible traffic violation or other reason. As a passenger, even if such an incident occurred, only I, the driver, would be carded and maybe cited. Highway patrol never had qualms with passengers, under normal circumstances.

We ended the day in Tucson, checking in, for the first time on this trip, in a nice place. I wanted to end our little odyssey with a sweet taste. It was a resort located on the northern side of the city, from where an incredible view of the surrounding mountains during the day and an amazing display of the city lights, down in the valley, at night was offered. I checked in under my name only, and Les followed me inconspicuously to the room.

In the morning on the third day, after a nice breakfast and without being in a hurry, we drove the last leg of the trip from Tucson to Nogales, the border city which, like Berlin used to be, is divided by a wall between the U.S. and Mexico. This wall divides between two cultures, between the best of the West and the Third World. It was a short one-hour drive on the only American highway I knew that showed distance signs and speed limits in kilometers, rather than miles, in preparation for the encounter with the Mexican roads and distance calculations.

Both of us smiled at the ironic coincidence appearing on our right side, about twenty miles south of Tucson, in Santa Cruz Valley. It was a museum located in what used to be the symbol of the Cold War, a symbol of the many billions of taxpayers money wasted on expensive, military toys, now relics. On our right, behind miles of artificial hills parallel to the highway, was the only remaining silo for the Titan 2 Intercontinental Ballistic Missiles. This was once one of the most top secret places in the States, one of the eighteen such silos that used to ring Tucson. Now, as a museum, it was the only one in existence, reminding of the days when these 100-feet tall, 170-ton monsters were standing erect in their launch ducts, behind 8-foot thick walls and 3-ton blast doors. Equipped with thermonuclear warheads, they were capable of reaching the main target, the former Soviet Union, in less than thirty minutes.

It was a timely reminder of the picture depicted by Les about the Cold War, the Pentagon, the military might, the fast changing generations of weaponry, and the shifting of the pendulum from enemies to friends and from fears of annihilation to cordial and normal relations, and vice versa.

The narrow road, splitting off from the highway and leading to what used to be the ultimate threat to our civilization, was crowded with tourist buses and RVs on their way to or from the museum.

Later on, while driving and chatting along the way, my eyes fixated on the road ahead, I asked Les, casually, what his plans for the future are. What followed was completely unexpected. He turned his head towards me and said;" I hope you are not going to make fun of me, Robert, but I intend to write a book."

"And what are you going to write about? Your life as a spy?" I asked him, with sarcastic humor in my voice, not anticipating his astonishing answer.

"Robert, I am going to write about a subject which has bothered me for many years."

Noticing my encouraging silence, he kept talking; "We spent our time talking about 9/11 events and I know you are convinced it is just a crazy 'conspiracy theory'. However, this national tragedy pales, when compared with the casualties, damages, ravages and devastation another operation brought on America. You'll probably classify it, as well, as a 'conspiracy theory'. But in this case I can give you at least one name as a witness.

My name.

I intend to write about the trade of arms for drugs. In both cases, Robert, the people behind these activities could not even imagine the magnitude of the end results, when their plans went wrong and got out of control."

Noticing the look in my eyes, Les said; "Don't look at me again as if I am crazy.

When I met you, many years ago, in the Washington airport, I told you about my ascent in the echelons of the Company and the high ranking position given to me. I did not tell you about some dark reasons behind these rewards. I can tell you now.

While in Central America, when the contras escalated their financial pressure on the American benefactors, I was exposed to a scheme different than the arms for hostages. It was a scheme of financing the contras operations with drug money. I witnessed first hand the beginning of a trade which exploded within few years and got completely out of control. What was in the early stages a small pipeline of drugs channeled into the States, mainly to the needy West Coast, resulted in the epidemic of crack cocaine. I saw planes landing on small strips, unloading arms and getting loads of drugs, arriving from South

America and transshipped to the States. You have to keep in mind that the people dealing in arms did it for one reason only; money. They were shady people, not the kind you want to introduce to your family. For them, drugs were just another way to maximize the profits.

To my great sorrow, I saw it happening and although I did not take any part in these despicable activities, I kept my mouth shut. In truth, there was not a lot I could do; too many high officials and high ranking politicians got involved and I did not have any chance to be heard. Even now, so many years later, I have doubts if my professional success was due to my qualifications or an attempt to bribe me, to keep me quiet."

I was taken completely by surprise. I turned my head slightly towards Les, without taking my eyes off the road and said; "My knowledge about this subject is very limited. I know, like many other Americans, the predilection of C.I.A., in its glorious days of combating communism in South Asia, to get mixed in the opium and heroin trade. I did hear of Air America, the notorious air pipeline, but not much else."

I was telling the truth and it showed, because Les said; "Robert, you are still so naïve. The Company has been involved in so many big time drug smuggling operations, we, the insiders used to say its initials stand either for Crack In America, or for Central Intoxication Agency.

Remember, I spent many years digging through its archives and I accumulated vast knowledge and information. But this ugly episode was not even a secret, although many wished it was. For a while it reached such public outcry that a special Senate Subcommittee, chaired by Senator Kerry, same one to become later a Presidential candidate, investigated the subject, back in 1989.

So, you asked me what my plans are and you got the answer."

He kept quiet for a long while and I did not want to disturb hid thoughts and memories. He seemed to be scrutinizing me and then, thoughtfully, he said; "Listen, Robert, I had a revelation."

"And what is it?" I asked obligingly.

"It's about you. I really underestimated your capability to fool other people."

I was wondering what he means, so I kept quiet, concentrating on the road ahead while he kept talking.

"You know, we people have the tendency to categorize others either as stupid or smart. But this is an oversimplification. The stupid ones have to be divided into two groups; the ones who are stupid, but they know it and act accordingly, and the ones who are stupid, but they think they are smart. On the other hand, the smart ones should be divided into two groups as well; the ones who are smart and act and behave accordingly, and the ones who are smart, but they hide under the cover of acting naïve, stupid, or clueless. They are the dangerous ones, getting whatever they want without being noticed.

Like you.

My hat off to you."

I smiled at the compliment, but the smile faded quickly when Les kept talking;

"However, Robert, you forgot something."

"What?" I asked.

"My axiom, Robert; no meeting is accidental in *our, and I mean our,* line of business. To this, I have to add another principle; whenever there is a doubt, there is no doubt-it's true."

I kept quiet, dumbfounded.

Nothing else needed to be said.

We completed the rest of the trip in complete silence.

I parked my car in one of the parking lots set up especially for the border crossers. We walked the last few hundred yards to the border. The only guards were the U.S. Customs, scrutinizing and checking the ones coming into the U.S. side. The entrance into Mexico was completely unregulated. No guards, security, or documents checks. Evidently, the Mexican authorities were not worried about illegal American immigrants trying to sneak inside and steal Mexican jobs.

I remained on the U.S. side.

Les passed through the narrow passage into the Mexican side under the eyes of the only, indifferent, Mexican guard manning it and quickly disappeared in the crowds of vendors trying to sell trinkets to the visiting Gringos. From there, he was supposed to reach Mexico City by bus, and then he was on his own.

No tears, no embraces, no handkerchief waving. Just a strong handshake, a thank you from him, a good luck from me, and he was gone.

About six months later I went on a vacation, with my wife, to Costa Rica. We took one of those eco-trip packages, where a chartered plane takes you to the northern airport of Liberia, half an hour away from the Pacific coast. There, a few resorts offered you plenty of food, entertainment, sun, and the opportunity to explore nature. We took a few day trips to see the volcano, Lake Arenal, horseback riding, and river boats in the forest jungle.

I did not tell my wife there was any reason to this trip and destination, other than just another vacation, but I was not entirely honest. I had steered and enchanted her with brochures and stories about the beauty of the country in a premeditated way.

I wanted to check one wild thought which had preoccupying my mind lately.

On the fifth day of our vacation I took a day trip by myself, leaving my wife in the company of some vacationers she had befriended there.

It was a tiring one, spending most of the day on a bus ride. Such rides are no fun on Costa Rica roads. Most of them have potholes and sinkholes, some of them impassable. These rides have to be taken on an empty stomach, otherwise your breakfast could haunt you.

It was a day trip to neighboring Nicaragua, visiting a few cities, mainly Granada and Masaya, the city with the large artisan market for local crafts.

The bus entered Nicaragua through the only land border passage on the Pan American Highway. From there it drove north toward Masaya. A few kilometers into the country, I noticed a road sign with an arrow indicating a left turn to San Juan del Sur. I approached the bus driver and the accompanying guide, I handed each a hundred dollar bill. I told them I want to stop and get out. On their way back, at 5:00 p.m., I told them I would be there waiting for them to stop and pick me up to take me back to Costa Rica and my hotel. They received the "regalo," the gift, gladly, but I was warned that if I am not there when they return, I am on my own.

I got out of the bus and waited at the intersection, another hundred dollar bill in my hand. It made the first vehicle passing by stop with screeching brakes, surprisingly fast for such an old rickety pickup truck.

I reached the beach in less than an hour from the moment I got out of the bus.

It had not changed much, other than the appearance of a modern, middle sized hotel and the disappearance of the billboard showing late President Somoza watching over his subjects.

It was mid week and the beach was not crowded. Some locals. A few European tourists, men in Speedo bathing suits tight enough to see their religion, with ladies exposing their bare breasts to the merciless sun. There were also some Americans, men in baggy knee-reaching shorts passing as bathing suits, restrained by their overweight companions to turn their heads to the wrong direction. I was wearing shorts, a T-shirt, my baseball cap, and sunglasses, which made me look like part of them, inconspicuous and generic.

In the distance, I saw him.

He was walking the beach with his slight, but unmistakable limp— my present to him.

He looked relaxed and at peace with himself and with the world.

While I was wondering if and how to approach him, his walk took him further away from me, and then he mingled with the others.

I spent a few more moments on the beach, watching the limping, aging man who replaced the young and agile one who had sprinted from the darkness and saved my life, not far away from where I was that moment.

I thought of his words, in the car, about accidental meetings which are not accidental and about doubts which are certainties.

I was trying to decide if Les, perhaps, saved me again from trouble by not sharing with me everything he probably knew.

Or, maybe, he fooled me once again like he did so many years ago in the same place, by getting out and away while using me, feeding me with small potatoes and keeping the fat meat to himself.

Or, maybe, he belonged, indeed, to a mental ward, and he used me to facilitate his escape.

My reveries were punctuated by the laughing cries of the seagulls circling above me.

I turned around and caught the first ride back to the highway, waiting for the bus to take me back.